Glessner House butler's pantry.

Prairie Avenue Cookbook

 *Recipes and Recollections from Prominent 19th-Century Chicago Families*

CAROL CALLAHAN

Southern Illinois University Press
Carbondale and Edwardsville

Printed in the United States of America
Edited by Teresa White
Designed by Joanna Hill
Production supervised by Natalia Nadraga
96 95 94 93   4 3 2 1

Library of Congress Cataloging-in-Publication Data

Prairie Avenue cookbook : recipes and recollections from prominent
   19th-century Chicago families / [compiled by] Carol Callahan.
     p.   cm.
     1. Cookery, American—Midwestern style. 2. Prairie Avenue
(Chicago, Ill.)—Social life and customs. 3. Prairie Avenue
(Chicago, Ill.)—History. I. Callahan, Carol.
TX715.2.M53P72 1993
641.5977—dc20   92-23088
ISBN 0-8093-1814-8 (cloth)   CIP
ISBN 0-8093-1815-6 (paper)

To Be a Good Cook

To be a good cook means the knowledge of all fruits, herbs, balms, and spices; and of all that is sweet in fields and groves, savory in meats. It means carefulness, inventiveness, watchfulness, and readiness of appliance. It means the economy of your greatgrandmothers and the science of modern chemists; it means much tasting and no wasting; it means English thoroughness, French art, and Arabian hospitality; it means, in fine, that you are to be perfectly and always ladies (loaf givers), and you are to see that everybody has something nice to eat.

— JOHN RUSKIN

Contents

Preface / xiii
Prairie Avenue Origins / 1
Victorian Food and Cooking / 9
Measures and Weights Used by Victorian Housekeepers / 17

 Breakfast Fare / 19

Egg Timbales / 19
Paris Eggs / 19
Eggs à la Sauce Robert / 21
Stirred Eggs / 22
Breakfast Oat Cakes / 22
Oat Cakes / 23
Buckwheat Cakes / 23
Sour Milk Waffles / 24
Rice Waffles / 24

Corn Cakes / 25
Corn Fritters / 25
Popovers / 26
Doughnuts / 26
Dainty Butter Rolls / 27
Hashed Potatoes in Cream / 28
Creamed Muffins / 29
Spoon Bread / 29

 Teatime Butters and Spreads / 31

Flower Butters / 31
Paprika Butter / 32
Chutney Butter / 32
Shrimp Butter / 32
Horseradish and Cheese
    Spread / 33
Date Spread / 33
Sardine Spread / 34
Lobster Salad / 34

Chicken Salad / 35
Potted Chicken for Traveling / 35
Brown Bread / 36
Bran Bread / 37
Lettuce Sandwiches / 38
Lemon Sandwiches / 38
Traveling Lunch Sandwiches / 39
Cucumber and Nasturtium
    Sandwiches / 39

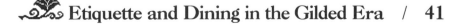 Etiquette and Dining in the Gilded Era / 41

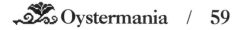 Soups and Garnishes / 47

Black Bean Soup / 47
Veal Broth / 48
Veal Gumbo / 48
Potage à la Reine / 49
Rabbit Soup / 50
Sorrel Soup / 51
Cream of Asparagus Soup / 51
Cauliflower Cream Soup / 52
Oyster Stew / 53

Cream of Leek Soup / 54
Green Pea Soup / 54
Mushroom Soup / 55
Corn Soup / 55
Chestnut Soup / 56
Sweet Potato Balls / 57
Egg Dice Timbales / 57
Cracker Balls / 58
Green Pea Timbales / 58

Oystermania / 59

Relish for Raw Oysters / 59
Panned Oysters / 59
Roasted Oysters / 61
Fried Oysters / 62

Scalloped Oysters / 62
Oyster Pancake / 63
Oysters Maître d'Hotel / 63
Pickled Oysters / 64

Fish and Seafood / 65

Lobster Newburg / 65
Trout in Aspic with Sauce
   à la Diable / 65
Sauce à la Diable / 67
Crab Flake Sublime / 68
Poached Salmon with Seafood
   Sauce / 69
Seafood Sauce / 69
Codfish Soufflé / 70
Baked Shad with Shad Roe
   Sauce / 71

Shad Roe Sauce / 72
Curry of Fish / 72
Halibut à la Poulette with
   Yellow Sauce / 73
Yellow Sauce / 73
Broiled Mackerel / 74
Fish au Gratin / 74
Fish Forcemeat / 75

The World's Columbian Exposition / 77

Poultry / 83

Galantine de Dende, Lucullus / 83

Roast Turkey with Bread
   Stuffing / 84

Roast Goose / 85

Apple Stuffing for Goose / 86

Chestnut Stuffing for Goose / 86

Potato Stuffing for Goose / 87

Quail on Fried Cornmeal
   Mush / 87

Fried Cornmeal Mush / 87

Potted Pigeon / 88

Pheasant Pie with Oysters / 89

Roast Partridge / 90

Breast of Duck / 90

Chicken Breasts with Poulette
   Sauce / 91

Poulette Sauce / 91

Creamed Chicken / 92

Mrs. Glessner's Chicken
   and Rice / 92

Meat and Specialty Dishes / 95

Young Roast Pig for Christmas / 95

Savory Beef / 96

Syrian Lamb / 97

Mutton Chops / 98

Meatballs / 98

Chicken Livers and Chestnuts / 99

Corn Beef Hash / 99

Kidneys with Potatoes / 100

Sweetbreads / 101

Risotto / 101

Risotto / 102

Pig's Feet à la S. Menehould / 103

Golden Birck / 103

Venison Steak / 104

Tamale Pie / 105

Servants / 107

Side Dishes and Salads / 113

Stuffed Onions / 113

Parsnip Fritters / 113

Tomato Pie / 115

Green Corn Pudding / 116

Broiled Mushrooms on Toast / 116

Stuffed Cucumbers / 117

Turkish Pilaf / 118

Asparagus / 118

Creamed Potatoes / 119

Sweet Potato Croquettes / 119

Potato Salad / 119

Asparagus Salad / 120

Celery Salad / 121

Chiffonade Salad / 121

Watercress Salad / 121

Jardinière Salad / 122

Tomato Jelly Salad / 122

French Dressing / 123

Tarragon Salad Dressing / 123

Mayonnaise Dressing / 124

Creamy Salad Dressing / 125

Cooked Salad Dressing / 125

Sauces, Pickles, and Preserves / 127

White Sauce / 127
Allemande Sauce for Beef / 128
Currant Jelly Sauce for Lamb / 128
Raisin Sauce for Ham / 129
Fruit Sauce for Ham / 129
Pickled Watermelon / 129
Pickled Beets / 130
Pickled Sweet Corn Ears / 131
Pickled Carrots / 131

Grated Cucumber Pickle / 132
Cold Tomato Relish / 132
Mushroom Catsup / 133
Oyster Catsup / 134
Whole Preserved Apples / 134
Spiced Peaches / 135
Rhubarb Marmalade / 136
Mincemeat / 136

Prairie Avenue Children / 139

Cakes / 145

Coconut Cakes / 145
Black Christmas Cake / 147
Angel Food Cake / 147
2nd Day Chocolate Cake / 148
English Walnut Cake / 149
Seed Cake / 150
Fruit Cake Blitz / 151
Individual Cheesecakes / 151

Turn-of-the-Century
   Cheesecake / 152
Updated Cheesecake Recipe / 153
Orange Cake / 153
Sponge Cake / 154
Huckleberry Cake / 155
Strawberry Shortcake / 156

Pies and Tarts / 157

Wheatless Piecrust / 157
Homemade Puff Pastry / 157
Cheese Tarts / 159
Banbury Tarts / 160

Lemon Chiffon Pie / 161
Apple Pie / 162
Apple Custard Pie / 162
Squash Pie / 163

# Pudding / 165

Charlotte Russe / 165

Indian Pudding / 166

Baked Indian Pudding / 166

Genoise Cream / 167

Ambrosia / 168

Cranberry Pudding / 168

Plum Pudding / 169

Lemon Rice Pudding / 170

Caramel Whip / 170

Apple Snow / 171

Afterthought Pudding / 172

Sunday Pudding / 172

Calling / 175

Cookies and Assorted Desserts / 181

Lemon Jumbles / 181

Vanities / 182

Hermits / 183

Hard Ginger Cookies / 183

Drop Ginger Cakes / 184

Orange Cookies / 185

Ladyfingers / 185

Chocolate Cookies / 186

Grandma Cookies / 187

Fudge Brownies / 187

Genuine Scotch Shortbread / 188

Delicate Gingerbread / 188

Gingerbread / 189

Omelette au Rhum / 190

Candy / 190

Nougat / 191

Ice Creams, Sorbet, and Dessert Sauces / 193

Nougat Ice Cream / 194

Carnot Sherbet / 195

Vanilla Ice Cream / 196

Chocolate Ice Cream / 197

Lemon Ice Cream / 197

Orange Ice Cream / 198

Raspberry Cream Ice / 198

Peach Ice Cream / 199

Grape Ice Cream / 200

Banana Sherbet / 200

Regents Punch / 201

Roman Punch / 201

Romaine Punch / 202

Theodore Thomas Punch / 202

Brandy Sauce / 203

Lemon Sauce / 203

Honey Love Sauce / 203

Prairie Avenue Household Formulas and Hints   /   205

Photographic Credits   /   209

Preface

Nothing seems nearer or dearer to home than recipes handed down from generation to generation. Mothers pass recipes to daughters, daughters-in-law, grandchildren, and great grandchildren. Thus ethnic, religious, and family traditions are carried on in the most intimate of ways: at our tables. The care taken to cook meals has long been equated with love, nurturing, the ideal of home and family tradition, and mealtime was and still is a valued and intimate family gathering.

The Victorian woman's domain was the home, and in this arena she held much authority. She alone was responsible for the moral, spiritual, and physical well-being of those in her home. Even in the homes of families of means with hired cooks responsible for preparing meals, the lady of the house determined menus and collected recipes from cookbooks and friends for use at her table. Among Prairie Avenue's wealthy families, wives were sufficiently involved with the work of the kitchen that they shared and recorded menus, recipes, and household hints. Many of the recipes in this anthology have been in use by their family of origin for decades, and thus have they survived.

These "receipts," as they were known at the time, survive from the period 1880–1910 and together with the historic anecdotes contained in the text have been gathered from the cookbooks, journals, letters, handwritten ledgers, newspapers, magazines, scrapbooks, reminiscences, and oral histories of the families mentioned and their servants. Most of these sources were found in the archives of the Chicago Historical Society, the Glessner House Museum, and the Chicago Architecture Foundation. Other invaluable sources include a number of recent books on the history of eating and technology of food and its preparation. Foremost among these are *Food and Drink in America* by Richard Hooker, *Food in History* by Reay Tannahill, *Dining in America* by Kathryn Grover, *Tales of the Table* by Barbara Norman, *The Dictionary of American Food and Drink* by John F. Mariani, and the enormously informative and entertaining *Eating in America* by Waverly Root and Richard de Rochemont.

The challenge of the historic recipe is formidable; women spent so much time cooking in the nineteenth and early twentieth centuries that recipes were often just lists of ingredients with no instructions and sometimes no measurements. In other cases ingredients are only mentioned in text-styled instructions. Add to that the fact that ingredients, cooking utensils, and appliances have also changed, and it can become quite a mystery to make Grandmother's favorite recipe. What, for example, is a calf's rennet? Exactly how much is a handful of sugar, teacupful of flour, or wineglassful of sherry? Recipes were written for vegetables not yet bred into the jumbo, juice-filled specimens we now take for granted. What are a "spider" and a "quick oven"? The capabilities of modern ovens and microwaves further complicate translation.

Because I have tried to retain the quaint original language and authenticity of these historic recipes as much as possible, terminology in the instructions varies from one recipe to another. Where they did not already exist, I have added instructions or lists of ingredients with measurements to clarify recipes. These additions have been either enclosed in parentheses or included under "Modern Cooking Tip," which follows the original instructions for a recipe. A list of historic measurement translations found in *The White House Cookbook*, published in 1886, precedes the recipe chapters, providing a useful and entertaining dictionary of the unusual measurements used at that time.

This cookbook is the product of many years work by numerous individuals, all of whom volunteered their valuable time and creative effort. My deepest gratitude is extended to Jean Komaiko and Olga Davidson, the two women who researched most of the recipes and anecdotes and compiled an original manuscript that forms much of the body of this book. Without their inspiration and vision for this project, it could not have come to fruition. Equal thanks go to Kevin Morrissey and Barry Bluestein, who tested most of the recipes included in the text. I offer special thanks to Susan King for her constant help in preparing and reviewing this text during the two years spent on its refinement.

I also extend my gratitude to the following individuals for sharing their invaluable reminiscences of life on Prairie Avenue for this cookbook: Martha Batchelder, Katherine Shortall Dunbaugh, Mrs. D. H. Field, Bennet Harvey, Lydia Hibbard Holland, Margaret Keith Holloman, Mrs. Ray Klewar, Beatrice LaFargee, the Meeker family, Mrs. Robert Peck, Katherine Field Rodman, Harrington Shortall, Jack Simmerling, and Katherine Anderson Sulzberger.

Finally, to all of the many hearty souls who baked and cooked and tested recipes for months, ensuring that the contents of this book would be usable to our readers, I extend substantial thanks and credit. They are friends, relatives, and colleagues: Janet Alberti, Helen Anderson, Margaret Balanoff, Barry Bluestein, Anne Callahan, Lynn Callahan, Scott Davis, Bridget Gallagher, JoAnn Kaiser, Susan King, Margie McKelvey, Ann Maroney, Kevin Morrissey, Ann Pfister, Christina Prasinos, Melissa Rosengard, Cassandra Smith, Mary Kay Stangle, Tina Strauss, Diane Tiepner, Jody Vogel, and Paul Wellman.

I invite you to enjoy the product of the efforts of all of these individuals who believe in preserving and continuing the best of nineteenth-century tradition and the personal expressions of home and family recounted in these recipes and recollections.

Prairie
Avenue
Cookbook

Prairie Avenue Origins

"This country is just beginning to be astonishing," stated one American newspaper in 1879. The Industrial Revolution inaugurated an era of unprecedented growth and change that forever altered the fabric of American life. Population shifted from rural areas to urban centers, and the workplace from agrarian to industrial. Among American cities, Chicago itself was a phenomenon, growing at a rate never before witnessed in human history. Incorporated in 1837 with only four thousand residents, the young city struggled under the strain of 1.1 million people by 1890. Always noted for its incredible energy and drive, the city emerged as the railroad center of the nation following the Civil War, supplying goods to settlements in growing midwestern and western communities. By the 1880s the Chicago River had become one of the busiest ports in the country.

It was in this environment that mammoth fortunes could be amassed nearly overnight as the opportunities of entrepreneurship created by industrial growth were seized by energetic individuals. Chicago's industrialists were bold gamblers who bought and sold their businesses during the hours of the Great Fire in 1871 in hopes of making fortunes or cutting losses on buildings and inventory that might or might not burn. In 1889 these same leaders undertook the monumental task of changing the course of the Chicago River to eliminate sewage flow into Lake Michigan, a feat later called by city residents the "eighth wonder of the world."

In 1892 the *New York Tribune* estimated that there were four thousand millionaires living in the United States. In cities all across America grand residential avenues emerged to house the mansions of these wealthy captains of industry. In expression of their aspirations, these individuals commissioned homes designed by fashionable ar-

1. From *Land Owner* magazine, 1874, which featured the first article promoting Prairie Avenue.

chitects in styles mirroring those of European nobility. Nearly every city had one such grand residential street; New York's Fifth Avenue, Washington, D.C.'s Massachusetts Avenue, Los Angeles's Wilshire Boulevard, Detroit's Woodward Avenue, Buffalo's Delaware Avenue, Cleveland's Euclid Avenue, Rochester's East Avenue, New Orleans's St. Charles Avenue and Richmond's Monument Avenue were among them, but none boasted as much consolidated wealth in just a few blocks as did Chicago's Prairie Avenue.

During the 1860s a large middle class began to emerge in America with resources to spend on the vast quantities of manufactured products then coming into the marketplace. At this same time, Prairie Avenue developed into a comfortable, sparsely populated middle- and upper middle-class neighborhood of grand Italianate homes with ample lawns and elegant rowhouses. Just one block to the east lay the inlets and marshes of Lake Michigan's shore. The street was unsurfaced, dusty in summer and often muddy during the rains of spring and fall. Across this sometimes treacherous roadway, resident William Hibbard laid an elevated path of stepping stones across which his wife, Lydia, could travel to visit her friend Mrs. Shortall across the road. Cottonwood trees and elms shaded the walks and the houses, and produce sprouted in kitchen gardens.

In October of 1871, a mammoth fire consumed central portions of Chicago, advancing in deadly swathes through residential sections to the north, west, and south. Although Prairie Avenue itself was untouched by the fire, many of its residents played a critical role in the phenomenal rebirth of the city that was to follow. With two companions and a team of horses, John Shortall journeyed to his office in the midst of the inferno and removed property deeds and titles to the relative safety of his home. These records provided the foundation for the Chicago Title and Trust Company, which aided the reopening of businesses and reconstruction of buildings as soon as the ashes of the fire had cooled. Shortall's neighbor, William Hibbard, co-owner of the city's largest hardware company, transported records and stock to the family home, where living space gave way to commercial enterprise. By the time the fire was finally over, Hibbard & Spencer was ready to supply hardware from the Prairie Avenue home of the firm's founder for the rebuilding of the city.

This Great Fire did not interrupt Chicago's rapid population growth, and Prairie Avenue began to change. The city's popular affluent neighborhood just west of the business district was becoming

2. Prairie Avenue looking south from Eighteenth Street, showing the William Kimball house *in the left foreground,* ca. 1905.

increasingly crowded by growing numbers of immigrants, and many Chicago businessmen began seeking other residential locations more convenient to their workplaces. They looked favorably on the near South Side, attracted to the available land ripe for building and a neighborhood unencumbered by Chicago River crossings over notoriously unreliable, busy bridges. City horsecar lines and the Illinois Central Railroad provided easy transit from the business district to this near South Side neighborhood. As Chicago rebuilt itself from the ashes of the Great Fire, such eminent citizens as Marshall Field, George Pullman, and Philip Armour cast appraising eyes over likely sites for new homes—settling their collective gaze upon Prairie Avenue. Almost immediately, the street became a magnet.

Gone were the stepping stones trod by Mrs. Hibbard and Mrs. Shortall; Prairie Avenue was surfaced in cobblestone. Street lighting was installed. As fortunes were amassed, imposing Second Empire-style mansions with mansard roofs and conservatories were built beside Queen Anne confections and elegantly ornamented French chateaux, intermingled with the more modest Italianate homes of an earlier era. Elaborate iron fences now surrounded many of the properties, and the splash of fountains echoed through summer gardens.

"If you want to see the richest half-dozen blocks in Chicago, . . . drive down Prairie Avenue from Sixteenth Street to Twenty-second. Right there is a cluster of millionaires not to be matched for numbers anywhere else in the country," announced the *Chicago Herald* in 1887. Indeed, Prairie Avenue, or "Palace Avenue," according to one newspaper, had become home to many of the city's most influential leaders: Marshall Field, George Pullman, Philip Armour, William Kimball, Samuel Allerton, Joseph Sears, and John Glessner. So popular was the burgeoning residential area after Chicago's fire that by 1885 there were no more sites on the street left for development. By 1893, the year of the popular World's Columbian Exposition, residents of the city's most fashionable street enjoyed the neighborhood's zenith.

The fate of Prairie Avenue was augured by the very factors that had made it a desirable place to live. Within little more than a decade after the World's Columbian Exposition, prominent Chicago families began moving to the city's newly fashionable North Side neighborhoods as noise and dirt from expanding nearby commuter rail lines just blocks to the east interrupted residential quiet. Residences be-

3. Marshall Field's house at 1905 Prairie Avenue, ca. 1895, designed by Richard Morris Hunt. The little boy riding the pony in front of the house is probably Marshall Field, Jr.

gan to give way to commercial activity because of the neighborhood's proximity to the city's business district. During the early 1900s many of Prairie Avenue's grand homes had become high-class rooming houses. Nearby south Michigan Avenue hosted a strip of automobile showrooms, and just a few blocks away on State Street was the city's red-light district. By the 1920s only a handful of the street's prominent residents remained in their Victorian homes. During the next two decades many of these houses would fall to the wrecker's ball to make way for warehouses and small factories.

In 1966, a group of enterprising architects turned this tide of events by founding the Chicago Architecture Foundation to save the home of industrialist John J. Glessner, built on Prairie Avenue by famous American architect Henry Hobson Richardson. Since that time, Prairie Avenue has found new life as a historic district, due to the efforts and vision of the Chicago Architecture Foundation and the city of Chicago. The home of John J. Glessner was opened as a house museum in 1971 and is now the only Richardson-designed residence in America that is restored and open to the public. This historic district also boasts the city's oldest building, Clarke House, built in 1836, which is also open to the public as a museum. Together these museums and historic district recapture the distinctive social world of Chicago's first families, who helped build Chicago into the city it is today, and whose lives and culinary traditions are the subject of this cookbook.

4. Glessner House entry hall looking into the parlor.

Victorian
Food
and Cooking

‽"American" cuisine is an enigma, borrowed from so many different sources that origins are often blurred. Much of Native American cooking was adopted by early settlers in the New World, including such foodstuffs as pumpkins, beans, corn, oysters, and turkey. The wealth of immigrant groups who came to America in the nineteenth century contributed colorful culinary traditions as well. From the French have been gleaned chowders, derived from the word *chaudiere*, and cheeses. German immigrants brought with them frankfurters and weinerwurst. The Pennsylvania Dutch created "shoofly pie," and the Shakers' "oyster pie" and "corn oysters."

The nineteenth-century American diet was probably the most diverse in the world as the bountiful landscape expanded with settlement and cultivation to produce seemingly endless quantities and varieties of fruits, grains, vegetables, milk, and livestock. Four hundred million acres of virgin soil were planted between 1860 and 1900, providing an unparalleled supply of food. The meals prepared with these harvests were simple by our standards—made from home-produced grains and sugar processed from sugar beets, lard, rich creams gleaned from fresh milk, and butter churned from these creams. As the century progressed, Americans grew less of their food, preferring to buy foods that were difficult to raise and process. Flour and sugar in particular became popular purchases, and refined white sugar began to replace other sweet alternatives like honey, molasses, and maple sugar.

Oysters had been common fare in the New World since the arrival of the first settlers; rich oyster beds off the eastern seaboard provided a plentiful supply of large specimen up to a foot in length. Because of this plenitude, they were also cheap, as noted in British traveler

Charles Mackay's book *Life and Liberty in America* (1859): "The rich consume oysters and Champagne; the poorer classes consume oysters and lager beer, and that is one of the principal social differences between the two sections of the community." Americans' passion for oysters did not abate with westward expansion. Oysters were transported on stagecoach lines from Baltimore to Ohio, and on canal boats to western destinations to meet this demand. Canned and pickled oysters were available as far west as St. Louis by 1856. They were served every way imaginable: creamed, fried, baked, grilled, flaked, minced, roasted, scalloped, cutleted, stewed, and raw on the half shell, and new ways of preparing them were invented with regularity. This demand so depleted eastern oyster beds by the 1880s that they eventually became a delicacy, as they remain today.

Annual consumption of red meat, particularly of pork and beef, was unmatched in early nineteenth-century America. During his trip to Europe in 1878, Mark Twain envisioned utopia: "a mighty porterhouse steak an inch and a half thick, hot and sputtering from the griddle; dusted with fragrant pepper; enriched with little melting bits of butter of the most unimpeachable freshness and genuineness; the precious juices of the meat trickling out and joining the gravy, archipelagoed with mushrooms; a township or two of tender, yellowish fat gracing an outlying district of this ample county of beefsteak; the long white bone which divides the sirloin from the tenderloin still in its place." Americans bravely ate all kinds of meat products: pigs' heart, liver, and feet; lamb's heart, feet, and tongue; beef tongue and kidneys; calf's brains; and turtle lungs.

By the later part of the nineteenth century, French cooking was introduced and soon became the latest fashion. From this regional tradition a great repertoire of exotic game (song and field birds—such as lark, snipe, plover, grouse, partridge—and terrapin) entered fine American restaurants and dining rooms, as did seafoods covered with rich, sweet sauces. So popular was French cooking in fashionable restaurants and chic homes of late nineteenth-century America that it became the fare of choice at Chicago's World's Columbian Exposition. Not everyone appreciated the confusion caused by menus composed of strange foreign words. "Isn't it a pity," quipped one grumbler, "that our own rich language is inadequate to the duties of a fashionable bill of fare?" Insinuations were offered that chefs and stewards without knowledge of French simply wrote down the unknown words as they heard them repeated.

Technological developments during the nineteenth century increased the range of foods available and expanded options for its preparation. Preservation techniques using ice and the development of canning and refrigeration made the transport of perishable foods over long distances viable on faster clipper ships and even speedier trains. Thousands of pounds of ice had been artificially manufactured in America and exported internationally since the early part of the nineteenth century, an enterprise dominated by "Ice King" Frederick Tudor of Boston. Produced on flooded farm fields in winter, ice was chopped, well insulated in straw and sawdust, and stored underground. Steamships successfully delivered ice-packed fish as early as 1820, and the great blocks of "fine, clear ice" were transported from Massachusetts to China and Calcutta in the 1830s. The first simple icebox, an ice compartment beneath a food storage compartment, was developed as early as 1803, and by the 1820s "icemen" delivered essential ice blocks to households to service this convenience, which had replaced root cellars as the preferred means of food storage. The icebox was heralded as a "convenience no family should be without" in one 1840 cookbook, and "a necessity of life" by *Godey's Lady's Book* in 1850.

The invention of the first mechanical refrigerator in 1834 correlated with the invention and patenting of ice-making machinery, securing the growing role of refrigeration in preserving foods. By the 1840s milk could be shipped across the country by rail, and Chicago received its first lobster by rail amid great fanfare, which arrived, newspapers reported, "as fresh as could be desired." Pineapples and coconuts regularly arrived on ships from Cuba, the West Indies, and Central America in the 1860s. Meats packed in ice could be successfully transported by sea and by 1877 were shipped frozen halfway across the globe. Restaurants had their own ice-making machinery, and the advent of the refrigerated boxcar encouraged long-distance shipment of foodstuffs. Humble bananas presented the greatest shipping challenge, requiring such delicate transport that they were not commonly available in this country until the 1870s, at the exorbitant cost of one dollar each. Thus did fruit became an out-of-season treat, giving rise to the custom of tucking a fresh orange in children's Christmas stockings.

Other innovations in food preservation included the mason jar, invented in 1858, which allowed the preservation of vegetables and fruit for out-of-season consumption. Meat, fish, fruit, and vegetables

5. Clarke House dining room.

safely preserved in heated, sealed cans were generally available by the 1860s; one decade later Americans were happily consuming thirty million cans of these goods annually. By 1885 Bordens sold sealed bottles of pasteurized milk.

More precise cooking equipment such as the cookstove, or closed-top woodburning stove, replaced open hearths and primitive brick ovens by 1840, allowing for the first time precise adjustment of cooking temperatures by using a series of flues, dampers, and metal plates. These advances expanded flexibility and accuracy in food preparation, particularly in baking, as did the advent of baking soda (called "saleratus"), baking powder (1856), and commercial yeast (1868). By the later part of the nineteenth century, the cookstove had evolved into quite sophisticated, precise iron ranges and gas stoves.

The science of nutrition lagged behind cooking technology, resulting in some dangerous concoctions. Recipes instructed cooks to boil pickles with copper pennies to keep the pickles green, use sulphuric acid to make vinegar, poisonous cherry laurel to imitate almond flavoring, and red lead to color Gloucester cheese. The discovery of bacteria by the Pasteurs in the 1860s opened new doors to the understanding of disease and ended such unsafe practice as the consumption of diseased meat.

Vitamins were discovered in 1886, allowing for further improvements in diet. Condensed milk, first produced in the 1850s, contained sugar, which impeded bacterial growth. "Butterine," an 1860s butter substitute, was developed from suet, chopped cow udder, and a little warm milk. First commercially produced in 1873, this strange mixture eventually evolved into the product now known as margarine.

Interest in healthful eating blossomed by the century's end. Horace Fletcher espoused "fletcherism," chewing each mouthful of food thirty-two times, once for each tooth, for proper digestion. His theories won such prestigious followers as John D. Rockefeller, William James, and Thomas Edison. Dr. John Harvey Kellogg of the Western Reform Institute at Battle Creek supported his dictum—"Bran does not irritate. It titillates!"—by developing a coarse bran food called "granose" to strengthen his patients' teeth. Later renamed "Toasted Corn Flakes," 100,000 pounds of the cereal were sold in the first year of production. Kellogg's patient Charles Post jumped on the bandwagon and created the healthful drink "Postum" in 1895. He followed this success with a new breakfast cereal, "Elija's Manna,"

6. Glessner House: kitchen looking into butler's pantry.

which sold well once renamed "Grape-Nuts," securing his role in the breakfast cereal industry and giving rise to another long-lived favorite: "Post Toasties."

Compilations of recipes assembled in the late eighteenth and early nineteenth centuries, called "cookery books," "recipe books," or "receipt books," helped women keep up with the changes in foods, techniques, kitchen utensils, and cooking equipment created by industrialization. The first cookbooks were aimed largely at middle-class, amateur cooks and helped them improve both the quality and ingenuity of their cooking and advised on the nutritive balance of their menus. By mid-century, cookbooks were published for professional chefs as well as for household use.

Some of the landmark cookbooks of the last century are *Miss Beecher's Domestic Receipt Book*, published in 1846, the first cookbook to attempt the definition of general cooking techniques. The English cookbook *Book of Household Management,* by Mrs. Isabella Beeton, published in 1861, was the first to estimate cost, quantities of food required, and preparation times of foods. Perhaps the most groundbreaking of all was the 1896 publication of *The Boston Cooking School Cook Book* by Fannie Merritt Farmer, which defined for the first time precise systems of scientific weights and measurements for ingredients, replacing imprecise terminology like the "dash," "pinch," or "handful" so common to cookbooks of the period and ensuring consistency in food preparation.

These books often espoused moral statements regarding food preparation. Mrs. Isabella Beeton asserted in her book that "a good meal should be fuel for the spirit as well as for the body." Mrs. Horace Mann's cookbook, *Morality in the Kitchen,* published in 1861, maintained "there is no more prolific cause of bad morals than abuses of the diet." Certainly the most useful advice provided in a Victorian cookbook comes from Dr. N. T. Oliver's 1894 cookbook: "Without *cleanliness* and *punctuality* good cooking is *impossible.* . . . A Good Cook *wastes nothing.* An hour *lost in the morning* must be run after *all day.* . . . Stew *boiled* is Stew *spoiled.*"

By 1890 all of the progress and convenience of "modern" food preparation had traveled full circle. In evidence once again that you truly can't please all of the people all of the time, noted Victorian gourmet Theodore Child longed for the old days, bemoaning, "In these days of progress, science, gas-stoves, sophistication, and democracy, the gourmet's dream is to taste real meat cooked with real fire, and to drink wine made with real grapes." Alas.

7. The Glessners' house on Prairie Avenue.

Measures and Weights Used by Victorian Housekeepers

This list from *The White House Cookbook* (1886) has been included for historic interest; however, some of the conversions listed below are not those currently used. I advise the use of the conversions included in each recipe when cooking the historic recipes in this cookbook.

4 Teaspoonfuls equal 1 tablespoonful liquid.

4 Tablespoonfuls equal 1 wineglass, or half a gill.

2 Wineglasses equal 1 gill, or half a cup.

2 Gills equal 1 coffee-cupful, or 16 tablespoonfuls.

2 Coffee-cupfuls equal 1 pint.

2 Pints equal 1 quart.

4 Quarts equal 1 gallon.

2 Tablespoonfuls equal 1 ounce, liquid.

1 Tablespoonful of salt equals 1 ounce.

16 Ounces equal 1 pound, or a pint of liquid.

4 Coffee-cupfuls of sifted flour equal 1 pound.

1 Quart of unsifted flour equals 1 pound.

8 or 10 ordinary sized eggs equal 1 pound.

1 Pint of sugar equals 1 pound. (White granulated.)

2 Coffee-cupfuls of powdered sugar equal 1 pound.

1 Coffee-cupful of cold butter, pressed down, is one half pound.

1 Tablespoonful of soft butter, well rounded, equals 1 ounce.

An ordinary tumblerful equals 1 coffee cupful, or half a pint.

About 25 drops of any thin liquid will fill a common-sized teaspoon. 1 Pint of finely chopped meat, packed solidly, equals one pound.

A set of tin measures (with small spouts or lips), from a gallon down to half a gill, will be found very convenient in every kitchen; though common pitchers, bowls, glasses, etc., may be substituted.

Breakfast Fare

Egg Timbales

Anderson Family Recipe

Makes 4–6 servings.

6 eggs beaten together
2 cups milk
Salt to taste
1 teaspoon onion juice
1 teaspoon chopped parsley

(Combine eggs with milk and seasonings), pour into cups (buttered 2-inch timbale molds or a buttered 9-inch ring). Put in pan with (hot) water and bake in oven like custard (in a 325-degree oven for 15–20 minutes, or until the tip of a knife inserted comes out dry). Serve with white sauce (see recipe, page 127).

The Prairie Avenue home of Bishop Anderson was the destination of visiting clergymen from around the world, who made it their temporary quarters in Chicago. If British, they typically left their boots outside the bedroom door, not knowing that the "bootsboy" who polished them was one of the bishop's four daughters.

Paris Eggs

Makes 4–6 servings.

6 eggs
1 teaspoon onion juice
Pinch of cayenne pepper
1 teaspoon salt
½ cup cream

The 1891 Maverick Cookbook, published by the Maverick Congregational Church of Boston, contained this homage to the egg: "O Egg! Within thine oval shell, / What palate-tickling joys do dwell!"

8. Frances M. Glessner and daughter, Frances, ca. 1886.

Boil eggs 20 minutes. Remove shell, cut in two, across (lengthwise). Remove yolks. Mix yolks into a smooth paste with the onion juice, red pepper (cayenne), salt, and cream. Fill whites with this and stand in bottom of baking dish. Pour sauce over and bake 20 minutes (at 300 degrees).

SAUCE

1½ cups cream
3 tablespoons cornstarch
1 small tablespoon butter
1 teaspoon salt
Pinch of cayenne pepper
1 teaspoon onion juice

Boil cream (i.e., in a double boiler over simmering water, heat cream to near-boil and whisk with cornstarch). Rub other ingredients together till smooth, put into boiling cream (mixture), and stir until thick and smooth.

Eggs à la Sauce Robert

Shortall Family Recipe

Makes 6–8 servings.
8 eggs, boiled 20 minutes
Hearts of 2 (medium) onions (about ½ cup, sliced)
1 tablespoon butter
1 tablespoon flour
1 cup stock (chicken broth)
¼ teaspoon salt
⅛ teaspoon pepper (white)
¼ teaspoon mustard (dry)

Slice the hard-boiled eggs (and set aside). Slice the onions and brown in the butter. Cook the flour in same; add stock slowly; season with salt, pepper, and mustard, and cook about 10 minutes (5 minutes if a

Prairie Avenue homes always had a crock of eggs in their storeroom. The following directions for preserving the best seasonal eggs are from the kitchen of Mrs. John Shortall: "Eggs are best in April, May and early June and these should be packed. They must be fresh, clean and unwashed. . . . Use 10 parts pure water (boiled and cooled) to 1 part silicate of soda solution. . . . Pack eggs, small end down, in crock or wooden tub, one layer, then cover with silicate of soda solution and repeat. Keep at about 50 degrees temperature. At 60 degrees temperature, they change. Will keep 3½ months and be good enough for meringue and angel cake. If perfectly fresh, will make an omelet after 6 months."

John Shortall was an animal lover in addition to a civic leader. In his concern for the treatment of horses, he distributed free copies of Anna Sewell's new novel, Black Beauty, to all city cabbies.

more runny sauce is desired). Mix the sliced eggs with this sauce, let them heat together about 2 minutes, and serve on platter.

 ## Stirred Eggs

According to Harvey family lore, a "dainty way to prepare an egg for an invalid" is to first beat it till very light, then season lightly, pour it over a slice of dry buttered toast, and steam covered for 2–3 minutes. "An egg prepared thus will not be likely to distress the weakest stomach."

Makes 6 servings.

1 cup gravy or consommé (chicken or veal broth; see recipe, page 48).
1 scant tablespoon butter
6 eggs beaten together lightly
6 slices buttered toast
Parsley to garnish

Heat a cupful of rich gravy or consommé in a saucepan in the butter, and melt it. When it boils, stir into it the eggs that have been beaten together just enough to mix whites and yolks. Stir 3 minutes over the fire, pour out upon hot buttered toast, and sprinkle with minced parsley.

 ## Breakfast Oat Cakes

Keith Family Recipe

Mrs. Eldridge Keith, who was known for her charity toward the poor, could often be found at her sewing machine making bloomers for children who did not live on Prairie Avenue. She confided to her granddaughter that she hoped Saint Peter was watching.

Makes 1–2 dozen oat cakes.

8 ounces (2 cups) oatmeal
1 teaspoon fat
Pinch of salt
⅛ teaspoon bicarbonate of soda
2 teaspoons hot water

Put oatmeal in bowl. Melt fat—bacon or goose is particularly good. Make a well in center of dry ingredients (oatmeal); put in fat and salt and soda and as much water so as to have a stiff paste. Make one bannock (cake) at a time. If you have a griddle, fine; if not, a flat bottomed frypan (cook over a medium heat,

ungreased, until brown on both sides). If not, cakes
can be made in the oven (bake at 400 degrees for 15
minutes). When served, are good spread with butter,
cheeses, fried herring, or sardines.

Modern Cooking Tip: The amount of hot water
needed may vary by one or two tablespoons depending
upon the oatmeal used.

Oat Cakes

Stirling Family Recipe

Makes 2–3 dozen oat cakes.
2 cups steel-cut oatmeal
1 cup flour
½ teaspoon baking powder
1 teaspoon salt
2 heaping tablespoons lard
½ cup cold water

Mix oatmeal, flour, baking powder, and salt together.
Melt lard and add it. Lastly, the water. Roll as thin as
possible. (Cut out cakes with a cookie cutter or 2½-
inch teacup.) Cook over a medium heat on a
ungreased griddle until brown on both sides.

Buckwheat Cakes

Glessner Family Recipe

Makes 2–3 dozen oat cakes.
¼ cup fine bread crumbs
1 cup scalded milk
⅛ yeast cake
¼ cup lukewarm water
¼ teaspoon salt
1 cup buckwheat flour

Perhaps no American food has as many names as the humble pancake, that ever-popular flat, griddle-fried breakfast food. Although all of these names are still in use: hoecakes, rice cakes, batter cakes, slapjacks, flapjacks, griddle cakes, flannel cakes, johnnycakes, journeycakes, Indian cakes, or Shawnee cakes, the word pancake *first came into general usage in the 1870s and has since become the predominant term for this favorite American food.*

After marrying and moving into her new home just one block from her parents, Frances Glessner presented her mother with the following poem, composed to elicit an invitation to breakfast.

Your Daughter's Complaint

A young ladies breakfast I've
   heard of
To be given by dear F. M. G.
An elegant party she, of
   course, always gives

But no "bid" is received by
  me . . .
As everyone's asked
Why can't I be too?
I'll send by acceptance,
With pleasure, to you
Oho Oh for a "bid". Oh! for a
  "bid"!
To the breakfast of F. M. G.
Many invitations have been
  sent out
But never a one to me.

*Following the poem, Frances
wrote, "Written invitation in
poetry required."*

*Sunday mornings were high
points of the week to many
Prairie Avenue children. To
Katherine Field Rodman,
they meant breakfast across
the street with Great Uncle
Marshall, where one could
feast on waffles with maple
syrup, and afterward roam
the great house or stand en-
tranced before a corner cabi-
net of bibelots from around
the world.*

*From a newspaper humor
column of the period: "How
do you like my waffles?"
asked the society matron.
"Could not be nicer, did you
make them yourself?" re-
sponded her guest. "Oh yes,*

1 teaspoon molasses
⅛ teaspoon soda
2 tablespoons lukewarm water

Soak bread crumbs in milk for 30 minutes. Dissolve
yeast cake in ¼ cup lukewarm water and add to milk
and bread crumb mixture. Add salt and buckwheat to
make a batter, thin enough to pour. Let mixture rise
overnight. In the morning stir and add the molasses.
Then dissolve ⅛ teaspoon soda and 2 tablespoons
lukewarm water and add to mixture. Cook same as
griddle cakes.

 ## Sour Milk Waffles

Makes about 1 dozen waffles.
5 eggs (separated)
1 quart sour milk (4 cups buttermilk)
2 tablespoons melted butter
1 teaspoon baking soda
Salt to taste
Flour enough to make a stiff batter (3½ cups)

Modern Cooking Tip: As cooking directions were
missing altogether for this receipt, we suggest that the
following steps be followed to prepare the batter for
the waffle iron: Beat egg yolks in a large bowl. Beat in
milk and melted butter. Sift flour, baking soda, and
salt into mixture, stirring constantly. Beat egg whites
until firm peaks hold; fold whites into mixture.

 ## Rice Waffles

Makes about 8 waffles.
Butter the size of an egg (¼ cup)
1 teacup (½ cup) boiled rice
3 eggs (separated)
1½ cups flour

1 cup milk
Pinch of salt
1 teaspoon baking soda
2 teaspoons cream of tartar

(Mix butter and rice.) If cold, warm rice on the stove.
Add the yolks well beaten; add gradually (sift in)
flour; add milk, a little salt, cream of tartar, soda, and
lastly, just before baking, stir (fold) in whites of the
eggs, well beaten (till peaks hold firm; cook in waffle
iron).

Corn Cakes

Harvey Family Recipe

Makes 1 loaf.
Butter half the size of an egg (3 tablespoons)
2 tablespoons sugar
1 egg
1½ cups sweet (whole) milk
Pinch of salt
2 teaspoons baking powder
1 cups white cornmeal
1 cup flour

Beat the butter and sugar to a cream (with an electric
mixer or by hand); into this break an egg, add milk,
salt, baking powder, corn meal, flour. Bake ½ hour in
a greased pan (in a 9-by-9-inch pan in a 375-degree
oven).

Corn Fritters

Harvey Family Recipe

Makes about 1 dozen fritters.
1 egg (separated)
1 pint grated corn (2 cups fresh or canned
kernels, lightly chopped)

indeed. I read off the recipe to the cook and turned the patent flour sifter all my myself."

The Ladies Home Journal *of 1890 contained the following instructions for "How to Drink Milk": "Why milk is 'distressing' to so many people as they commonly complain, lies in the method of drinking it. Milk should never be taken too quickly, or too much at one swallow. If a glass is swallowed hastily, it enters into the stomach and then forms one solid, curdled mass, difficult of digestion. If, on the other hand, the same quantity is sipped, and three minutes are occupied in drinking it, then on reaching the stomach, it is divided, and proper digestion is obtained, as well as a most nutritious effect."*

1 tablespoon milk
½ cup butter
1 cup flour
Salt and pepper to taste

Fry in small cakes on a buttered griddle and brown well on each side (as you would a pancake).

Modern Cooking Tip: To prepare ingredients for frying: Beat egg yolk in large bowl. Add corn, milk, and melted butter. Sift flour into mixture, stirring constantly. Add salt and pepper. Beat egg white and fold in.

 *Popovers*

Shortall Family Recipe

Makes about 1 dozen.
3 large tablespoons flour
¾ pint (1½ cups) milk (about)
2 eggs, well beaten
½ teaspoon salt

Add enough milk to the flour and salt to make a smooth, stiff batter. Add the beaten eggs and enough more milk to make it the consistency of soft custard. Beat all well. Pour into buttered muffin tins and bake 45 minutes at 375 degrees.

 *Doughnuts*

Meeker Family Recipe

Makes 2–3 dozen doughnuts.
1 cup sour milk (buttermilk)
1 teaspoon baking soda
2 eggs, well beaten
1 cup sugar (¼ cup reserved)

At breakfast one morning, the parting of guests Mr. and Mrs. Jack Gardner of Boston was described by an observer as follows: Mr. Gardner informed his wife, "I am dining out tonight, Isabella." "So am I" she rejoined. "I shall be home late," he continued, to which she answered, "I shall be later."

Deep-fried yeast pastry arrived in America with the Pilgrims, who had acquired the tradition from Holland in the seventeenth century. These first doughnuts were holeless, small balls, or "nuts" of dough. By the mid-

1 tablespoon melted lard (or ½ tablespoon each
melted lard and butter)
Pinch of salt
Flour enough to roll out (1¾ cups)
⅓ cup vegetable shortening
1 teaspoon cinnamon

Modern Cooking Tip: The Meeker cook would have
prepared the doughnuts in a manner such as follows:
Mix together milk, baking soda, eggs, ¾ cup sugar,
shortening, salt, and flour to form well-blended dough.
Cover lightly and let stand 20 minutes. Roll out on a
lightly floured board until ½ inch thick; cut with 2–
2½-inch doughnut cutter. In a heavy frying pan, heat
vegetable shortening to 360 degrees. (If not using a
thermometer, flick a tiny drip of water into the oil; if
it crackles, the oil is ready. (Do not let oil smoke.)
Place 3–4 doughnuts at a time into hot oil for about 1
minute, or until golden brown; flip and cook the same
on other side. Using slotted spoon, remove from oil
and drain on paper toweling. While warm, sprinkle
with reserved sugar and cinnamon mixed well.

Dainty Butter Rolls

Glessner Family Recipe

Makes 2 dozen.
2 cakes compressed yeast (½-ounce size)
1 tablespoon sugar
¼ cup milk (scalded and cooled)
1 tablespoon vanilla
3 egg yolks
½ cup butter
1½ cup flour
¼ cup sugar
¼ cup fine chopped nuts (walnuts)

Dissolve yeast and sugar in milk, then add the vanilla

dle of the nineteenth century, holes were commonly cut into the center of doughnuts using such available small round utensils as sewing thimbles, which made the confection convenient for dunking into coffee. Doughnut cutters soon followed, appearing in catalogs by the 1890s.

In the old leisurely days on Prairie Avenue, marketing was undertaken by the mistress of the household and was an excuse for informal trysts with peers. Arthur Meeker, Jr., remembered his grandmother being told by a friend, "Now, Kate, I'm off to New York and shall buy a dress that will be right for me to wear to market."

and well-beaten yolks. Cut butter into flour and combine the mixtures. Form into small 2-inch balls and place in cheesecloth. Set in pan, add warm water until the dough is completely submerged, removing them after a minute (to hasten the rising of the dough). Let balls stand 1 hour before removing from cloth. Roll dough into pieces about 4 inches in length and twist. Put into well-greased pan. Dust with mixture of ¼ cup sugar and ¼ cup chopped nuts. Let rise 20 minutes. Bake in hot oven at 400 degrees for 15–20 minutes.

Modern Cooking Tip: Dried yeast may be substituted for compressed yeast.

Hashed Potatoes in Cream

In an era of hearty breakfasts, hashed potatoes in cream were a regular and often an accompaniment to broiled salt fish. According to one descendent, "they were so good you wanted to cry."

This breakfast treat is very creamy, so it is suggested that hard biscuits be on hand to absorb the cream.

Makes 6–8 servings.

4 cups pared, coarsely chopped raw potatoes
1 teaspoon flour
1 teaspoon salt
¼ teaspoon pepper
1 pint (2 cups) of half milk and half cream (Half & Half)
1 tablespoon butter
1 teaspoon chopped parsley

Put potatoes into a stewpan with flour, salt, and pepper. Mix these materials lightly and add (Half & Half). Set the stewpan into another containing boiling water (or place mixture in double boiler) and cook the mixture until it gets boiling hot—say about 12 minutes. Then add butter and parsley. Remove the stewpan from the water and set it where its contents will boil up once. Taste, to be sure that there is enough seasoning, then serve.

❧ Creamed Muffins

Field Family Recipe

Makes about 1 dozen muffins.

4 eggs (separated)
½ cup flour
1 pint (2 cups) cream
Pinch of salt

Beat whites (to a soft peak) and yolks separately; mix flour, cream, salt, and yolks together, then stir (fold) in whites. Bake in a quick oven (425 degrees in greased individual muffin tins) for 20 minutes.

❧ Spoon Bread

Field Family Recipe

Makes 1 loaf.

Enough sweet milk to make a thin batter (2 cups whole milk)
½ teaspoon salt
1 cup cornmeal
½ tablespoon butter
½ tablespoon lard
2 teaspoons baking powder
4 eggs beaten together

Bring milk and salt to a boil; reduce heat. Stir in cornmeal and continue to cook until mixture begins to thicken. Add butter and lard; when melted, remove from heat. Stir in baking powder and beaten eggs. Pour into a greased (9-by-10-inch Pyrex) pan and bake in a 375-degree oven for about 45–50 minutes.

It is reputed that when Mrs. Marshall Field attended one of the celebrated dinner parties in the Prairie Avenue home of the Hibbards, followed by a game in the Hibbards' tenpin alley, she remarked, "Oh Mrs. Hibbard, I didn't think one could have such a good time without dancing."

9. Glessner House parlor.

Teatime Butters and Spreads

These turn-of-the-century butters and spreads add an elegant touch to teatime fare. Their preparation is easy, especially when a food processor is used to cream the butter or cream cheese. Refrigerate before serving, as this helps fuse the flavors.

Flower Butters

Can be made when fresh flowers are abundant; spread on delicate bread they are much appreciated served with fruit salads at five o'clock teas. Advantage is taken of the fact that freshly churned butter readily absorbs odors and flavors.

The butter is cut into thin slices of good size and so arranged that most of the surface is exposed to the air, they are then put in large tight jars or boxes with a quantity of petals of rose, violet, honeysuckle, nasturtium, or any flower fancied and kept tightly closed for several hours, or until the flowers are withered. With the more delicately flavored petals, it may be necessary to repeat the operation to obtain the desired result.

Spread the butter on thin slices of bread, placing 2 buttered sides together and cut into squares, triangles, or fancy shapes. Arrange in a folded napkin in order to preserve the odor. Ornament with same variety of flower used in flavoring the butter.

Pink roses became the decoration of choice at receptions and teas during the 1880s and 1890s, and rose theme teas were a must for every socialite. The all-time winner of these rose extravaganzas must have been the 1885 coming-out party of a Prairie Avenue debutante. Several hundred ladies arrived to this occasion sporting "elaborate carriage dresses" to find rosebuds in "loose bunches on the mantel . . . on small tables and pinned to the portieres . . . coming out of the gas brackets, and a hundred rosebuds on the main table."

Modern Cooking Tip: Make sure that the flowers you use are pesticide-free and have not been sprayed with chemical substances. Beware of flowers like lilies of the valley and star of Bethlehem, which can be poisonous.

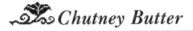 *Paprika Butter*

2 tablespoons butter
½ teaspoon paprika

Cream butter and mix with paprika. Use this with thinly sliced marinated cucumber for sandwiches. Specially good with whole wheat bread.

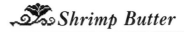 *Chutney Butter*

2 tablespoons butter
1 tablespoon chutney (chopped if coarse in texture)
¼ teaspoon prepared mustard
½ teaspoon lemon juice

Cream butter and mix well with other ingredients.

Shrimp Butter

This subtle delicacy is actually made from the shells of cooked shrimp. It's quite good on French bread toasted lightly under the broiler, as well as on baked potatoes.

12 boiled shrimp
1 ounce (2 tablespoons) butter

Pick the meat from the shells of boiled shrimp; dry (the shells) and pound them in a mortar, adding good

No Prairie Avenue household would be found without its copy of Manners and Social Usage *for advice on social etiquette. Author Mrs. Sherwood espoused the following recipe for successful dinner conversations: "Polite, humorous, vivacious, speculative, dry, sarcastic, epigrammatic, intellectual, and practical people all meet around a dinner-table, and*

butter. Then place it in a saucepan on a moderate fire for about 5 minutes, stirring until it clarifies. Strain (into a bowl) through a napkin (or a double-thickness cheesecloth) and let congeal.

Modern Cooking Tip: Shrimp shells may be pureed in the food processor.

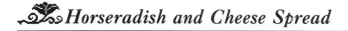Horseradish and Cheese Spread

3 ounces cream cheese
1 tablespoon cream (optional)
1–2 tablespoons fresh horseradish, grated (to taste)
½ teaspoon lemon juice (if using fresh horseradish)
Salt to taste
Dash of paprika

Cream the cream cheese and add cream if dry. Mix all ingredients well.

Modern Cooking Tip: Bottled horseradish, if substituted for fresh, must be drained.

Date Spread

½ cup dates, chopped
½ cup walnuts, chopped
½ cup whipped cream
A few drops lemon juice

Mix all ingredients well. Spread on buttered whole wheat bread.

much agreeable small-talk should be the result."

# Sardine Spread

½ cup mashed sardines
½ teaspoon Worcestershire sauce
⅛ teaspoon onion juice
A little butter if needed

Mix together, if dry, add enough butter to make of right consistency to spread.

Lobster Salad

It was a banner day in 1842 when Chicago received its first lobster, which was shipped by rail to Cleveland, where it had to be boiled and then sent on by boat. The Daily America *reported that it was "as fresh as could be desired," and that the gourmets of the day were "set on edge."*

Makes 4 servings.

MARINADE
½ cup vinegar (white)
½ cup oil (good quality olive oil)
Juice of 2 lemons (½ cup)
1 teaspoon salt
½ teaspoon white pepper

Put this over boiled lobster meat (enough to serve four) and set it in a cold place (refrigerate to chill).

SALAD
1 pint (2 cups) marinated lobster meat
3 hard-boiled eggs, cut lengthwise and across
2 (ripe) olives, cut fine
½ tablespoon minced dill pickles
½ tablespoon smallest capers
¼ cup mayonnaise

Toss the lobster meat and the other ingredients together and cover completely with mayonnaise. Toss lightly but thoroughly. (Refrigerate.)

❧ Chicken Salad

Originally developed by the Kinsley Catering Service in 1871.

Makes 2¾ cups.

2 cups (cooked) white chicken meat, minced
¾ cup chopped celery
Yolk of 1 raw egg
1 hard-boiled egg (separated)
1 teaspoon salt
1 teaspoon pepper
½ teaspoon mustard (Dijon)
1 tablespoon salad oil
1 tablespoon white wine vinegar
Celery leaves, green pickles, and pickled beets for garnish

Combine the white meat of a chicken with the weight in celery an hour before wanted. For dressing, break yolk of hard egg very fine with silver fork and add yolk of raw egg, salt, pepper, and mustard, working all together smoothly. Add gradually salad oil and vinegar. Mix chicken with dressing, pile in dish, and garnish with delicate leaves of celery, white of egg cut into rings, green pickles cut into slices, pickled beet root.

Modern Cooking Tip: Since current nutrition practice cautions against eating raw eggs, this ingredient can be safely omitted from this recipe, if desired.

❧ Potted Chicken for Traveling
Harvey Family Recipe

Makes about 4 cups.
4 cups chicken meat (chopped and cooked)
¼ cup diced ham
¼ pound (½ cup) butter

One young visitor to the World's Columbian Exposition encountered an elderly man exiting one of the fair's exhibit halls. Overwhelmed by the 1,037 acres of the fair, the tired old gentleman exclaimed to her in despair, "I can't see the damn thing in a month!"

⅛ teaspoon salt
⅛ teaspoon pepper

Take a roasted fowl and carve off all the meat. Take 2 slices of ham and chop it with chicken. Add to this best butter, salt, and pepper, now pound this altogether to a paste. Put the mixture in a jam pot, cover closely. It will keep in a cool place 10 days or long enough for any moderate journey. This is an agreeable relish and makes a pleasant luncheon when traveling.

Modern Cooking Tip: Mixture may be pureed in the food processor. We advise that this salad be kept refrigerated despite the author's assurance that it will keep for 10 days without refrigeration.

 ## Brown Bread

Meeker Family Recipe

This hearty baked bread is a variation of the steamed brown breads with which we are more familiar.

Makes 1 loaf.
2 cups graham (whole wheat) flour
1 cup white flour
2 teaspoons baking soda
1 teaspoon salt
½ cup cornmeal
¼ cup sugar
1 cup raisins
2½ cups sour milk (buttermilk)
¼ cup molasses
1 egg

(Sift flours, baking soda, and salt together. Stir in cornmeal, sugar, and raisins.) Add liquid to dry ingredients. Pour into a buttered (8½-by-4½-by-2½-inch) loaf pan; fill ⅔ full. Let stand 1 hour. Bake in a moderate oven (325 degrees) for 1 hour.

Bran Bread

This bread has dense texture with robust whole wheat flavor. It is best when sliced very thin.

Makes 1 loaf.

2 packages dry yeast
2 cups bran flour
1 teaspoon salt
About 4 cups white flour (2 cups reserved)
1 teaspoon sugar
1 cup warm mashed potatoes (1 large or 2 small potatoes)
2 cups potato water (water in which potatoes were boiled)

Stir the liquid into the dry ingredients. Cover bowl with cloth (plastic wrap and a towel). Permit to double in bulk. (Let rise in a warm place until doubled, about 1 hour. Punch down dough.) Place in greased pans (shaped into 2 loaves and place into well-greased 8½-by-4½-by-2½-inch loaf pan). Permit to rise again till (almost) double in bulk. (Brush bread tops with water.) Bake in moderate oven for about 45–50 minutes (at 350 degrees until internal temperature is 190 degrees on an instamatic thermometer).

Modern Cooking Tip: Quick rise yeast will suffice. To blend the liquid and dry ingredients in the modern kitchen, which is a somewhat more involved process than the original recipe would indicate: In a food processor fitted with metal blade, combine yeast, bran flour, salt, 2 cups white flour, and sugar. Process to blend. Reheat potato water, if necessary, to 130 degrees. Combine with mashed potato. With machine running, drizzle mashed potatoes/potato water mixture through feed tube into dry ingredients. Blend in as much of the reserve 2 cups of white flour as is necessary to make a workable dough; additional flour may be needed. Turn out onto a floured board. Knead dough until it is smooth and elastic, about 10 minutes. Place in well-oiled bowl; oil all sides of dough.

Lettuce Sandwiches

When Prairie Avenue families went to polo games at the Onwentsia Country Club, they often had lettuce sandwiches and ice teas in the old pavilion.

Makes about ¼ cup.

1 teaspoon chopped onion
1 tablespoon vinegar
2 tablespoons olive oil
1 tablespoon lemon juice
½ teaspoon salt

Let the onions remain in the vinegar 5 minutes, then remove (and drain). Stir the ingredients together and spread lightly on crisp lettuce leaves laid between thin slices of bread and butter.

Lemon Sandwiches

Makes 1 cup.

1 cup butter
1 tablespoon French mustard (Dijon)
A little hot water if needed
Pinch of cayenne pepper
Yolk of 1 egg (hard-boiled)
2 tablespoons lemon juice
¼ teaspoon salt

Delicious sandwiches to accompany hot or cold tongue, also to eat with game or chicken, may be made by slicing thinly and evenly a loaf of good wheat bread and another loaf of Boston brown bread, each at least 24 hours old, and spreading the slices with a preparation made as follows: Take butter and mustard and make into a paste, adding a little hot water (if needed); add a pinch of cayenne pepper, rubbed together with the yolk of an egg and lemon juice. Rub the mixture together until it forms a smooth paste, adding more salt, if required. Having spread the mixture evenly and smoothly on the bread, make some of the sandwiches of 1 slice of wheat bread and 1 of the brown bread, the others all of wheat bread. Trim the edges evenly and cut them diagonally. Serve in a basket or fancy dish.

Traveling Lunch Sandwiches

Makes 1 cup.

½ cup sardines, chopped fine
½ cup ham, diced
Small quantity chopped pickles (1 tablespoon dill pickle relish)
1½ teaspoons mustard (Dijon)
¼ teaspoon pepper
1 tablespoon catsup
¼ teaspoon salt
½ teaspoon white wine vinegar

Mix sardines, ham, and pickles with mustard, pepper, catsup, salt, and vinegar. Spread between nicely buttered bread slices and cut in slices crossways. Will keep fresh for some time.

Cucumber and Nasturtium Sandwiches

Makes about 1½ cups.

2 cucumbers
1 nasturtium leaf
½ teaspoon onion juice
¼ teaspoon cayenne pepper

Before the advent of window screens, a fly whisk was kept on hand at Prairie Avenue dining tables. In the Hibbard household, a plain whisk was employed for everyday use, and one made of peacock feathers was used when guests were present.

Tucked into Mrs. Gibson's poets' album from 1884 was the following newspaper article carefully clipped from the Philadelphia Bulletin:

The Ideal Woman

She has no history.
Not only is she easy to live

with but she is worth living for.

She is too clever to talk of woman's rights, she takes them.

She is not such a fool as to fancy that any one is ever convinced by argument.

She wears frocks that match her hair, she does not dye her hair to match her frocks.

She helps her husband to build up a future for himself, and never seeks to rake up the past.

She does not believe that a man can love only once or only one. She herself prefers loving much to loving many.

She knows that when men talk about a woman being good-looking, they mean that she is well-dressed, though they do not know it.

She does not insist upon her husband eating up the cucumber sandwiches left over from one of the parties; she eats them herself and suffers in silence.

She knows that every real woman is the ideal woman—the fact being that every idea of ideal woman is wholly dependent on the idealist and every woman who is idolized is idealized.

Her ambition is to live up to her best photograph.

Enough creamed salad dressing to spread easily (½ cup)

Peel and split cucumbers lengthwise. Scoop out soft center with a teaspoon, chop remainder fine. Add a little onion juice, red pepper (cayenne), and salad dressing. Butter 2 thin slices of Boston brown bread. Spread 1 with mixture, lay a nasturtium leaf over it, and put other slice of bread on top. Don't let stand, will lose crispness. Boston brown bread, with a filling of nasturtium leaves and minced celery mixed with mayonnaise, makes another sandwich.

Etiquette and Dining in the Gilded Era

"Brutes feed. The best barbarian only eats. Only the cultured man can dine. Dining is no longer a meal, but an institution," asserted *The American Anthropologist* in 1888. Indeed, dining and etiquette were inextricably linked in the late nineteenth century, and table manners were the supreme test of refinement and character, or "good breeding," in the parlance of the day. The richness of this "gilded era" was reflected in the lavishness of the board and the intricacy of etiquette that governed social behavior for grand occasions.

Formal dinners consisted of fifteen or more courses and progressed from dishes of lesser importance to those that were richer and more lavishly prepared. Each of the numerous main courses was accompanied by a different wine. A hierarchy even developed among cutlery: the utensil of greatest refinement was the fork, to be chosen wherever possible over the lowly knife, whose blade was always to be kept out of one's mouth. Formal dinners generally lasted an hour and ninety minutes to two hours, after which guests remained in conversation for at least an hour to avoid exciting comment that they had come only for the meal.

Tea also became a popular and lavish social event, which acquired its own rules of menu, specialized utensils, and furniture. Tea was served accompanied by a boggling array of tea cakes, muffins, waffles, preserved fruits, and biscuits. A more formal tea, or "high tea," required the addition of meats to the menu, such as chicken, partridge, cold meats, and oysters, prompting Agnes Morton, author of *Etiquette*, published in 1868, to comment that "the gradations by which the frugal tea passes into the superabundant supper are not easily classified."

10. Glessner House dining room.

Dozens of etiquette manuals were published during the nineteenth century to support the obsession with formal dining, laying the groundwork for rules of polite table manners that still govern society, albeit less rigidly. Guests were expected to arrive punctually; never later than fifteen minutes after the requested time of arrival. More grievous yet would be to arrive early, "excit(ing) the suspicion that you came so early to make sure of the feast—a certain sign of greediness," according to one etiquette manual from 1868.

Such manuals advised on every aspect of behavior at the table, including dress, posture, seating arrangement, topics of conversation, and, of course, table manners. In abbreviated summary, one must control sounds, gestures, emotions, and necessary bodily functions and not eat loudly, quickly, take large spoonfuls, or neglect to use utensils, "scrape the last morsel of food from your plate," "rattle their chair," or "press against the table and shake it at every movement of your body," adjust themselves or clothing at the table, or pin their napkin over your breast "like an alderman or a slobbering infant." A diner feeling the urge to cough or sneeze was advised to excuse oneself and leave the table to accomplish the task. Neither were diners to comment on the food set before them, even in praise, a sign of "animal and sensual gratification" over "intellect . . . and . . . moral nature."

In this proper social atmosphere, visiting political, intellectual, literary, musical, and artistic celebrities became frequent dinner guests on Prairie Avenue when visiting Chicago—from the archbishop of Canterbury to Oscar Wilde. The Glessners' close friend Chicago Symphony conductor Theodore Thomas frequently brought such mercurial talents as guest artists Enrico Caruso and Ignace Paderewski to dine with the Glessners in their Prairie Avenue home. The strains of the full Chicago Symphony Orchestra resounded through their home on at least one occasion: a surprise concert in honor of the Glessners' twenty-fifth anniversary. It was said that only on Prairie Avenue was a thirty-foot tablecloth a necessity.

Formal social events on Prairie Avenue were lavish. Mrs. Marshall Field played impressario to a Mikado Ball in 1885 celebrating the seventeenth birthday of Marshall Field, Jr., which was reputed to cost $75,000. Decorators descended on the Field residence, transforming it into a Gilbert and Sullivan set with Koko's garden in the entrance hall, and bamboo, ivory, tapestries, and Oriental foliage throughout the house. Young guests arrived in wigs and Oriental

11. Joseph Sears dining room, 1815 Prairie Avenue, ca. 1885.

costumes and danced to the music of Johnny Hand's popular orchestra. Sherry's, the caterer, transported food and silver from New
York in two private railroad cars for the Fields' five hundred guests.
Twelve-year-old Ethel Field's friends dominated the dance floor until
11:00 P.M., when young Marshall and his peers took over.

Two thousand guests were invited to Florence Pullman's wedding
in her father's stately Prairie Avenue mansion, later described in
newspaper accounts two columns long. During a wedding reception
at the Keith family's house, eighty-five guests at a time partook of
creamed chicken, salted almonds, petit fours, and wedding cake in
the drawing room, where children had sequestered themselves from
the din on small chairs under the piano. Since the groom's family
produced breakfast cereals, the Keith boys arranged for the de-
parting newlyweds to be showered with puffed wheat.

Life was never to be quite the same again. The fortunes amassed
and abundance of goods available for consumption had dictated a
more formal and opulent lifestyle with specific codes of behavior for
Victorians of means.

12. John W. Doane House entry hall, 1827 Prairie Avenue, ca. 1884.

Soups
and Garnishes

❦ Black Bean Soup

Columbian Exposition Cookbook

Makes 8–10 servings.

1 cup black turtle beans (dried)
12 cups (3 quarts) water
3 pints (6 cups) beef stock
Salt and pepper to taste
1 saltspoon (¼ teaspoon) cloves
1 saltspoon (¼ teaspoon) allspice
1 wineglass (¼ cup) port or sherry
1 small lemon, sliced
1 hard-boiled egg, chopped

Soak beans overnight in cold water (to cover). Drain
and add water enough (12 cups) in the morning to
cook thoroughly (simmer, cover slightly ajar, at least 3
hours, or until beans split). One hour before dinner
(drain), rub through a sieve, and stir in plain beef
stock. Season with salt and pepper, cloves, and
allspice. (Simmer, covered, for ½ hour.) Just before
serving, add port or sherry. Also, lemon and hard-
boiled egg (for garnish).

Modern Cooking Tip: A food processor can easily
replace a sieve in the preparation of the bean puree.

*After traveling to Mexico,
Alice Hamlin Glessner de-
scribed a Mexican delicacy
called "pulque" to members
of the Monday Morning
Reading Class. "It has a hor-
rid, sour smell, looks like
watered milk, and tastes like
a combination of buttermilk
and garbage. The pulque is
the juice of the plant (ma-
guey cactus) when flowering,
which it does every seven
years. It is taken to town in
pigskin bags on the backs of
donkeys. They say the pulque taste, like the taste for
bull-fights, can be ac-
quired," which, we may
safely assume, she never
did.*

Veal Broth

This basic white stock is a component of numerous soup and sauce recipes.

Makes 5–6 cups.
Knuckle of veal (about 4 pounds)
½ teaspoon salt
12 cups water
2 carrots (sliced)
1 turnip (about ½ pound, sliced)
1 medium onion (chopped)
3 sprigs parsley (chopped)
3 leeks (about 1½ pounds, white and green portions, well washed)
2 tablespoons leaves of celery

Cover knuckle of veal and salt with water, boil, and skim scum (boil 8–10 minutes and ladle off residue that will rise to the surface until clear). Add carrots, turnip, onion, parsley, leeks, leaves of celery. Boil (simmer) 6 hours. Skim. Strain (and cool). Store.

Modern Cooking Tip: Veal neck bones may be substituted for a knuckle of veal; use at least 4 pounds.

Veal Gumbo

Makes 6–8 servings.
2 pounds fresh veal (shoulder or precut stew meat)
1 pound fresh pork (shoulder or roast)
½ pound okra (fresh or frozen)
½ cup chopped onion
¼ cup chopped parsley
2 pints (4 cups boiling water, half reserved)
Salt and pepper to taste
2 gills of claret (1 cup red Bordeaux or other dry red wine)

The senior class of the cooking school at the Woman's Refuge enthusiastically displayed their cooking skills by serving luncheon to the ladies of the board on December 27, 1894. The luncheon fell "on one of the worst days of the season . . . [and] only a very few were present." Those few were not disappointed, however, to be served a meal of tomato soup with browned crackers, breaded veal with browned sauce and olives, corned beef hash, macaroni scalloped, mashed potatoes, celery salad, bread pudding, doughnuts, and coffee. "Those present say that the luncheon prepared was delicious," reported the Refuge Journal *in 1895.*

Soup appeared with regularity on Prairie Avenue dining tables, served steaming hot in great tureens—bisque or potage, as thin as bouillon or as thick as gumbo; cream, chowder, or clear, braced with sherry or graced with timbales. This recipe is a modified gumbo to suit northern and midwestern taste.

Cut the veal finely, also the pork. Fry until brown.
Then cut the okra into small slices; add that with
onions and also parsley to the meat, stir until brown.
Add (2 cups boiling) water, flavor with salt and
pepper. Let it simmer slowly; in 20 minutes add
(reserved) water and claret wine. The soup is now
ready for the table.

Potage à la Reine

This is a puree soup in the manner of potato, cream,
or bean soup, but instead thickened with the paste or
puree of pounded chicken and rice.

Makes 8-10 servings.
3 cups cooked chicken meat
1 cup boiled rice
**2 quarts (8 cups) of chicken broth (fresh or
canned)**
½ whole nutmeg (or 1 teaspoon ground nutmeg)
**1 sprig of fresh thyme (or about ½ teaspoon dried
thyme)**
1 pint (2 cups) cream or milk
Salt and white pepper to taste

Procure a pound, or 3 solid cups, of clear (white)
chicken meat tender enough to mash to a paste, either
from 2 or 3 young chickens roasted or a large fowl
boiled. Mince it fine, pound it smooth, add the rice to
it while pounding, pour in some of the broth to
moisten it, then rub it through a perforated tin gravy
strainer or a sieve. The broth should have a piece of
broken nutmeg boiled in it and, if obtainable, a sprig
of green (fresh) thyme; and after that be strained. Mix
it boiling hot with the puree of chicken and rice. Set
on bricks or at the back of the stove to keep hot
without boiling (cover and simmer) and boil the cream
(or milk) separately and pour it in at last. Season with
salt and white pepper.

Modern Cooking Tip: In lieu of pounding and straining, the chicken and rice puree can be made in a blender or food processor by using the on-and-off pulse and adding liquid as needed.

Rabbit Soup

In the Stanley Field and other Victorian households, marrow bones were a delicacy, sometimes served as a separate course. Marrow was extracted from the bones with spoons designed for this purpose by English silversmiths.

Makes 8–10 servings.

2 rabbits (5 pounds total), cut up
Knuckle of veal or beef (about 2 pounds) or 1–2 slices bacon
4 quarts (16 cups) water
2 sliced onions
1 tablespoon flour
1 bunch each of parsley, thyme, and sweet basil (about 1 tablespoon fresh or 1 teaspoon dried of each)
6 cloves
12 grains whole allspice
Few blades (about 1 teaspoon) mace
Salt and pepper to taste
2–3 slices toast

Cut up rabbits as for frying, put this with a knuckle of veal or beef or slice or two of bacon into the soup kettle; cover with water, boil gently until reduced (1½–2 hours), and skim carefully until the broth is clear. Fry onions light brown color, stir into the onion the flour until it browns, and add to the soup; season with parsley, thyme and sweet basil, cloves, allspice, mace, pepper, and salt. (Simmer additional 20 minutes.) Toast thin slices of light bread and lay in the bottom of the tureen, pour on the soup, and serve hot, after removing the bones from the soup. Squirrels are good used in the same way.

Modern Cooking Tip: Use of bacon or 3–4 ounces of smoked turkey, rather than the knuckle of veal or beef, will produce a smoky taste.

 Sorrel Soup

Makes 6–8 servings.

1 cup sorrel
1 medium head lettuce
1 teaspoon chopped chervil
4 tablespoons butter (3 tablespoons reserved)
3 pints consommé (6 cups of chicken or veal
stock; see recipe, p. 48)
Pinch of sugar
2 cups croutons

Wash a good handful of sorrel and chop up together
with a lettuce; add chopped chervil and put in a
saucepan with 1 tablespoon butter. When beginning to
color lightly, add consommé, and boil gently 20
minutes. Add sugar and skim the grease carefully
from your soup. Serve with small squares of bread
(croutons) fried in (reserved) butter a light brown.

 Cream of Asparagus Soup

Makes 4–6 servings.

2 bunches asparagus
2 quarts (8 cups) water
1 pint sweet cream (2 cups light cream)
1 ounce (2 tablespoons) butter
2 tablespoons cornstarch
1 leaf mace (¼ teaspoon)
½ teaspoon salt
1 small wineglass (1½ ounces) sherry

Boil asparagus in water until very tender (about 20
minutes), then put through cullender (colander) (to
puree). To this add 1 pint of asparagus water (2 cups
of the water in which asparagus was boiled) and let
boil slowly (until thick). Boil the cream, melt the
butter, and add to above; thicken with cornstarch and
add salt. Just before serving in tureen, add sherry.

When an unexpected visitor to the Anderson household would stay for lunch or dinner at the bishop's invitation, his wife would waylay a daughter and tell her in whispers to add a cup of water to the soup.

Modern Cooking Tip: Asparagus may be pureed in the food processor after boiling. Be careful not to overcook.

Cauliflower Cream Soup

Makes 6–8 servings.

1 pint (about 2 cups) cooked cauliflower
1 quart (4 cups) soup stock (fresh or canned chicken broth)
½ blade (about ¼ teaspoon) mace
1 tablespoon minced onion
1 pint rich milk (2 cups Half & Half)
Salt and white pepper or cayenne pepper to taste
Flour and water mixed to a paste (to thicken, optional)
1 tablespoon butter
1 tablespoon minced parsley

The cauliflower is to be the principal article. Cauliflower left over from a previous dinner can be used. If to be cooked for the purpose, pick the cauliflower into little branches (flowerettes) and boil it separately in salted water nearly or quite half an hour. Boil stock with the mace and minced onion in (bring to a boil, then simmer for 10 minutes, or until onion is translucent). Mash (puree) about half of the cauliflower and put in; boil the milk and add that, season with salt and pepper. Thicken, if not thick enough already, with flour and water (water slowly added to 2 tablespoons flour until it forms a smooth, thick paste) till it looks like thin cream. Add the butter, the balance of the cauliflower branches whole as they are, and the green sprinkling of parsley.

Modern Cooking Tip: Cauliflower may be pureed in a blender or food processor; add liquid as needed. The soup can be thickened using cauliflower stalks that

The clear white broth that has had an old fowl boiled tender in it is best for such a soup as this. Any pieces or bones from the breakfast or dinner meats and a small allowance of any soup vegetables at hand may be put into the stock pot with it to make it richer.

have been boiled and pureed, or cornstarch, instead of
the traditional flour and water thickener. Cauliflower
does not need to be cooked as long as this recipe
indicates for puree, if so desired.

Oyster Stew

Makes about 4 servings.
**1 pint oysters with liquor (about 1½ pounds, or 18
oysters)**
1½ cups milk
½ cup cream
Butter for garnish

Cook the oysters (with liquor) and the milk (with
cream) in separate saucepans (over low flame; oysters
should be cooked until edges begin to curl, milk
brought to the boiling point). Dip the oysters from the
saucepan into the bowl they are to be served in, add a
ladle of milk and a small piece of fresh butter.

Modern Cooking Tip: The modern palate may
appreciate the addition of salt, freshly ground black
pepper, and cayenne pepper to taste. For a stew with a
stronger oyster taste, boil oysters and milk together in
a single saucepan just until oysters ruffle. (Be careful
not to overcook or oysters will have a rubbery
texture.)

FOR BOSTON FANCY STEW

To the above milk stew, add a slice of buttered toast
floating in it and the oysters on the toast. Use a large
shallow bowl, put the square of toast in it first, drain
the stew into it, and place the oysters neatly.

In 1914 young Frances Glessner fabricated a model of the famed Swiss quartette, the Flonzaley Quartette. Her handiwork was presented to the musicians at dinner one evening, an event remembered by her son: "It was covered with a large floral piece in the center of the table, which gave no hint as to what was underneath. . . . After dinner, the floral piece was removed with a flourish, and there, two feet from their noses, was this model of themselves playing! . . . For a moment nobody spoke, and then all four members of the quartette burst out in voluble language. . . . Each one of them pointed with delight to the eccentricities of the other three. I still remember Mr. Betti, with a magnifying glass peering over the shoulder of his own minature, trying to read the music on the music rack. It had been specially written by Frederick Stock, the conductor of the Chicago Symphony, in the style of Schoenberg, but was impossible to play—a fact which Mr. Betti soon appreciated."

In the first half of the nineteenth century, produce supplies in Chicago were limited. Families had winter and summer menus. It was big news, therefore, when the first out-of-season shipment of peas came into the city from New Orleans in 1852.

Cream of Leek Soup

Shortall Family Recipe

Makes 6–8 servings.

3 tablespoons butter (half reserved)
½ cup chopped onion
¼ cup chopped celery
4 cups chopped green portions of leeks
1 tablespoon flour
3–4 pints white stock (6–8 cups chicken or veal broth; see recipe, p. 48)
Salt and pepper to taste
½ bay leaf
1 clove
2 large or 3 small potatoes
3 cups chopped white portion of leeks
1 egg yolk, beaten (optional)
½ cup cream (optional)

Cook in butter (1½ tablespoons) an onion, a celery stalk, and the greens of 4 leeks cut fine. When partly cooked (limp), add flour, white stock, salt, pepper, bay leaf, clove, potatoes. Let cook 1 to 1½ hours (until potato falls apart). Cook by themselves in (reserved) butter the white parts of the leeks chopped fine. When soup is cooked, add the whites of leeks. At time of serving, add the beaten egg yolk and cream and cook briefly (for a thicker, richer soup).

Green Pea Soup

Makes 6 servings.

1 quart (about 4 cups) green peas (frozen, canned, fresh, or dried)
½ cup minced onion
2 tablespoons butter
1 tablespoon flour
1 cup cream

1 pint (2 cups) milk
Salt and pepper to taste
1 cup sour cream (optional)

Cover green peas with hot water and boil with onion until they can be easily mashed, 20 or 30 minutes. Cook together butter and flour until smooth, but not brown; add to the mashed peas and then add cream and milk. Season with salt and pepper and boil up once; strain and serve. A cup of sour cream added at the last moment is an improvement.

Mushroom Soup

Makes 6–8 servings.

¾ pint (about 1½ cups) fresh mushrooms, diced
5½ cups chicken or veal broth (see recipe, p. 48; 4½ cups reserved)
1 tablespoon flour
1 tablespoon butter
1 saltspoon (¼ teaspoon) salt
⅛ teaspoon pepper

Stew mushrooms in 1 cup seasoned broth (for 10 minutes). Add to this 4 more cups of stock. Thicken with flour rubbed into butter (melt butter and add flour, stir until butter is absorbed into flour but do not allow to brown; add remaining ½ cup stock reserved, emulsify [liquefy] into stock, and add to the large pot). Season with salt and pepper. (Heat about 5 minutes to serving temperature.)

The freshest mushrooms on Prairie Avenue came from the Harvey family, who grew mushrooms in their stable. Mushrooms were carefully bedded in the sweepings of the stable and tended by the coachman. Then they were gathered, broiled, and served under glass by the cook.

Corn Soup

Makes 6–8 servings.

1 pint (about 2 cups) grated corn (raw)
1 quart (4 cups) milk
1 slice onion

2 tablespoons butter
1 heaping tablespoon flour
Salt and pepper to taste

Cook the corn in a pint of hot water 30 minutes. Let the milk and onion come to a boil. Have the flour and butter mixed together and add a few tablespoons of boiling milk. When perfectly smooth, stir into the boiling milk; cook 8 minutes. Take out the onion and add the corn; season to taste and serve.

Modern Cooking Tip: Canned corn, cream-style or regular, which need not be cooked first, may be substituted; puree in a blender or food processor first.

Chestnut Soup

Mrs. Glessner once wrote in her journal that she had urged a reluctant guest to accept her invitation, because without her, there would have been thirteen at the table. The lady reportedly came, thus saving the occasion.

Makes 10–12 servings.
1 quart large chestnuts, (shells scored)
1 teaspoon salt
1 slice lemon rind
2 quarts (8 cups) chicken or veal broth (see recipe, p. 48)
1 wineglass (¼ cup) cream
1 tablespoon butter
1 tablespoon flour

Boil chestnuts for 20 minutes. Take off shells and skins. Put into saucepan with enough boiling water to cover them. Add salt and lemon rind. When soft (tender when pierced with a fork), rub through a sieve. Then pour over them, stirring all the time, the broth, cream, and the butter rolled in flour. Bring to a boil. Serve very hot.

Modern Cooking Tip: Chestnuts may be pureed in a food processor; if canned chestnuts are used, they do not need to be boiled first. Unsweetened canned chestnut puree may also be substituted.

Sweet Potato Balls

½ cup cooked sweet potatoes (skin removed)
1 tablespoon butter
Salt and pepper to taste
¼ teaspoon nutmeg
1 teaspoon grated cheese (Parmesan)
1 egg, beaten

Mash cooked sweet potatoes, season with butter, salt, pepper, nutmeg, and grated cheese. Moisten with beaten egg; roll into small balls and poach (in a 2-quart saucepan for 3 minutes, dropping mixture into boiling water by the heaping tablespoonful). Put the balls into the soup the last thing before serving.

Modern Cooking Tip: To prepare raw sweet potatoes, slice, put in covered dish, and cook in the microwave for 4 minutes. Cut away peel before mashing. These make a nice addition to veal broth or other broth soup.

Egg Dice Timbales
Shortall Family Recipe

2 eggs, beaten together
2 tablespoons milk
¼ teaspoon salt

(Beat ingredients together well.) Bake in a buttered (Pyrex) cup set in pan of hot water (water should come halfway up the side of the cup) till firm in center (at 325 degrees for about 30 minutes, or until knife comes out clean). When cold, cut in dice or prettily shaped pieces and pour soup over at serving time. Tastes good over thick soups.

Cracker Balls

For Ralph Waldo Emerson, hospitality consisted of "a little fire, a little food, and an immense quiet."

3 soda crackers (about 8 individual squares of the modern-size cracker, or enough to produce 3 tablespoons crumbs)
Butter the size of a hazelnut (1 tablespoon)
1 egg
Salt to taste
⅛ teaspoon nutmeg

Roll crackers as fine as flour. Mix with butter. Beat the egg and stir into the crumbs until smooth. Season well. Form into balls. Have soup boiling when you put balls in. Boil 3 minutes and serve at once. (These make a nice addition to broth soups.)

Modern Cooking Tip: Crackers may be crumbed in a blender or food processor.

Green Pea Timbales

½ cup mashed green peas
1 tablespoon soup stock (veal broth; see recipe, page 48)
Whites of 3 eggs
¼ teaspoon salt
⅛ teaspoon pepper
⅛ teaspoon nutmeg

Mix peas with soup stock and egg whites; season with salt, pepper, and nutmeg. Beat well together and place in a small (greased) mold. Set the mold into hot water (in a larger pan with the water coming halfway up the side of the mold) and place in a slow oven until the mixture is set (325 degrees for about 30 minutes, or until a knife inserted in the center comes out clean). When it is firm, cool and unmold, cut into small cubes, and put them in the soup just before serving.

Oystermania

❧ Relish for Raw Oysters

Makes sufficient sauce for 3–4 dozen oysters.

2 tablespoons finely chopped white onion
½ teaspoon salt
1 tablespoon horseradish
1 teaspoon English mustard
1 dozen drips of hot sauce (tabasco)
1 saltspoon (¼ teaspoon) white pepper
1 gill (½ cup) strong white vinegar

Mix all ingredients, let stand a few moments and put a very little on each oyster.

Modern Cooking Tip: To help open fresh oysters (which can also be opened by the vendor when purchased), place on dish a few at a time in the microwave and cook on high for 20 second increments, depending on the size and number of oysters.

"It seems almost unnecessary to give any directions for opening oysters," according to a nineteenth-century cookbook, "but I have seem them, poor things! So mangled, so mutilated, that I think a few words on the subject may be useful. . . . Remember, the bottom shell is the proper shell in which they should be sent to table; one generally in the country sees them served in the top shells, which is exceedingly provincial and absolutely wrong."

❧ Panned Oysters

Harvey Family Recipe

Makes 6–8 servings.

50 whole shucked oysters (about 2 pints, liquor reserved)
1 ounce (2 tablespoons) butter

13. Mrs. H. G. Hibbard.

2 saltspoons (½ teaspoon) salt
1 saltspoon (¼ teaspoon) white pepper
1 saltspoon (¼ teaspoon) mace
2 teaspoons whole allspice (ground)
Pinch of cayenne pepper
4 tablespoons cracker dust (¼ cup cracker
crumbs)

Put the oysters and their juice (liquor) into a bright
stewpan (nonaluminum), set on a quick fire; add the
butter, salt, and spices. Sift in the cracker dust, stir
gently till well mixed. At the first boil, pour them into
a hot tureen, cover, and serve immediately. If longer
cooked, they shrivel and get tough and indigestible.
They are often prepared in the same manner at table
in a chafing dish. Serve with toast.

Modern Cooking Tip: If there is insufficient natural
juice from the oysters, bottled clam juice may be used
to stretch.

℘Roasted Oysters

Allow 3–4 oysters per person as an appetizer, 6–8 per
person as a main course, adjusting proportions
accordingly.

Makes 1 dozen oysters.

1 dozen fresh oysters
2 tablespoons butter, cut into 12 thin slices
Salt and pepper to taste

Wash the shells well with a brush and cold water.
Place them in a pan (baking dish lined with
aluminum foil) with the deep half of shell down. Put
them into a hot oven (450 degrees) and bake until the
shell is well opened (10–12 minutes). Remove the top
shell carefully so as not to lose the liquor. Arrange
them on plates, and on each oyster place a piece of
butter and a little pepper and salt.

*In the Stanley Field house-
hold, roasted oysters were
served for special occasions.
There was even a special centerpiece to accommodate
them—mirrored at the bot-
tom, with bronze railings
around the sides, candela-
bra at both ends, and an
epergne filled with flowers
in the middle. Inside the
railings, the great object was
filled solid with roasted
oysters. Between every two
guests was a pail for
cracked shells.*

During a musicale at the Glessners, the guests made themselves comfortable throughout the many rooms of the house's spacious first floor. After the concert, a supper of hot oysters, salad, sandwiches, coffee cake, and ice cream was served by Charles Smiley, the caterer. "Mr. Keith," wrote Mrs. Glessner in her journal, "said he had never had as pleasant an evening out, because he did as he pleased."

Fried Oysters

Makes 3–4 servings.

2 dozen whole shucked oysters (about 1 pint)
2 cups cracker crumbs
4 eggs
4 teaspoons milk
Salt and pepper to taste
3–4 cups oil (vegetable or safflower, for frying)

Drain the oysters. Roll each one first in cracker crumbs, then in egg mixed with a little milk and seasoned with pepper and salt (the latter not necessary if using saltine cracker crumbs), then again in the cracker crumbs. Use first the crumbs, as the egg will not otherwise adhere well to the oyster. Place them in a wire basket and immerse in smoking hot fat. As soon as they assume a light amber color, drain and serve immediately. Oysters should not be fried until the moment of serving, for they are quickly cooked and it is essential to have them hot. Pickles, chowchow, horseradish, coleslaw, or celery salad may be served with fried oysters.

Modern Cooking Tip: In lieu of deep frying, oysters may be sautéed over a medium high flame for about a minute per side, until light golden in color. Put oysters into oil gradually so as not to lower heat level. For a lighter breading, substitute 1 cup of flour for 1 of the cups of cracker crumbs. Roll oysters first in the flour, then in egg mixture, and finally in the crumbs.

Scalloped Oysters

On cook's night out, scalloped oysters were a favorite dish, because they could be prepared ahead and popped in the oven by any member of the family.

Makes 3–4 servings.

2 dozen whole shucked oysters (about 1 pint, liquor reserved)
¼ cup bread or cracker crumbs
Salt and pepper to taste

3 tablespoons butter
Minimum 2 tablespoons oyster juice (liquor)

Place in a shallow, small baking dish a layer of oysters; over this spread a layer of bread or cracker crumbs. Sprinkle it with salt, pepper, and bits of butter; alternate the layers until the dish is full, having crumbs on top, well dotted with bits of butter. Pour over the whole enough oyster juice to moisten it. Bake in a hot oven (450 degrees) 15 to 20 minutes, or until browned. Serve it in the same dish in which it is baked; individual scallop cups or shells may also be used, enough for one person being placed in each cup.

Modern Cooking Tip: If there is insufficient natural juice from the oysters, bottled clam juice may be used to stretch.

Oyster Pancake

Makes 6 pancakes.
1 dozen whole shucked oysters (about ½ pint, liquor reserved), chopped
1½–2 cups milk
1 pint (2 cups) wheat flour
2 eggs
Pinch of salt

Mix oyster liquor and milk so that you have a pint (2 cups). Add wheat flour, oysters, eggs, salt. (Beat mixture.) Fry till nicely browned (on a lightly greased, heated griddle).

Oysters Maître d'Hotel

Allow 3–4 oysters per person as an appetizer, 6–8 per person as a main course, adjusting proportions accordingly.

At the Women's Refuge, a home for "fallen" impoverished young immigrant women, the forthright skills of sewing, cooking, and housekeeping were taught with added doses of Christian morality. "The event of the year," reported the 1895 newsletter, was the annual oyster supper, described as follows: "The girls arrayed in their best are served to supper and afterward devote the evening to singing, recitations, and as a special favor to dancing. Mrs. Gilbert sent us the oysters, a generous supply, and Mrs. Rae the pickles. . . . The girls contributed, and cake, candy, nuts and lemonade were served to twelve small girls, who afterward 'played with dolls.'"

Cocktail hour had not quite come into its day in the 1880s and 1890s in Chicago, as one can clearly see from the following concoction: "Emily Otis Cocktail: 1 jigger each of rum, gin, lemon juice, and maple syrup. Add a little fresh mint."

Makes 1 dozen oysters.

1 dozen whole shucked oysters (about ½ pint)
1 teaspoon butter
Salt and pepper to taste
Juice of ½ lemon (2 tablespoons)
Parsley for garnish

Dry oysters in a napkin (to absorb water). Put butter in handled pan of chafing dish (or skillet on stovetop); when it is very hot, add the oysters, sauté them a few seconds on one side, then on the other. (Be careful not to overcook or oysters will be rubbery in texture.) Season with salt and pepper; squeeze the lemon juice over the oysters, strew with a very little chopped parsley, and serve with or without toast.

Pickled Oysters

When in age Mrs. William Gold Hibbard was persuaded by her son to sit for her portrait, she consented reluctantly, and only on condition that he write one hundred times, on paper that she provided, "A fool and his money are soon parted."

80 fine oysters (3–3½ pints whole, shucked oysters, liquor reserved)
12 whole cloves
12 whole black peppercorns
12 blades (2 tablespoons) mace
2 small red peppers
2 small cups white vinegar
Salt to taste

Heat oysters and liquor in a porcelain-lined (nonaluminum) kettle. Just before they reach boil, take out oysters with a slit (slotted) spoon and set aside in jars. Add all the spices and peppers and heated vinegar to the liquor. Boil up once and pour while still scalding over the oysters in the jars. Cover and keep in a cool dark place (refrigerate). They will be ready to eat the next day.

Fish
and Seafood

❧ Lobster Newburg

Makes 4–6 servings.

4 tablespoons (¼ cup) butter
2 cups cooked diced lobster meat
½ teaspoon paprika
⅓ teaspoon nutmeg
3 egg yolks
1 cup cream
⅓ cup sherry
Salt to taste

To butter, add cooked lobster meat (in a saucepan over a low heat). Stir for 3 or 4 minutes and season with paprika and nutmeg. Add egg yolks and cream beaten together. Stir continuously for several minutes (until sauce begins to thicken). Add sherry and a little salt. Serve at once in patty cases with toast.

❧ *Trout in Aspic with Sauce à la Diable*

Makes 6 servings.

¼ ounce (1 packet) unflavored gelatin
5-pound trout
6¼ cups water (6 cups reserved)
1 cup vinegar (white)

At a reading of Faust *at the Glessners' house, for which twenty-five musicians from the Chicago Symphony Orchestra provided background music, Robert Lincoln and Allison Armour cooked lobster Newburg in a chafing dish for guests and members of the orchestra.*

BLUE POINTS

CELERY

—

CREAM OF TERRAPIN

—

PLANKED SHAD WITH ROE SAUCE

CUCUMBERS

—

FILLET OF CHAMOIS, SAUCE POIVRADE

STRING BEANS   SWEET POTATO CHATEAU

—

CARDINAL PUNCH

—

BROILED SQUAB

TOMATO AND CELERY MAYONNAISE

—

GLACES   CAKE

—

COFFEE   CRACKERS   CHEESE

AMONTILLADO   CHÂTEAU ROLLAND

MUMM'S EXTRA DRY

COGNAC   LIQUEUR

February 27th 1894. Mrs. Hammer

14. Hand-painted menu card from a dinner party given by Mrs. Harry Hammer in 1894.

½ lemon
2 bay leaves
2 tablespoons whole peppercorns
1 tablespoon whole allspice
1 large onion (sliced)
Parsley to garnish

(Dissolve gelatin in ¼ cup cold water and set aside.)
To about 6 cups of water add vinegar, lemon, bay
leaves, spices, and onion, and boil, adding fish after
about 5 minutes (water should just cover fish) to
poach. When the fish has boiled tender (about 8
minutes), pull off all the skin and fins. Split and lay
flat on a fish platter (removing all bones). To the
water in which the fish was boiled (poached) (strained
and reduced to 3 cups), add the gelatin that has been
soaked in cold water. When the gelatin is thoroughly
dissolved (take off heat and set in cold water (or chill)
until thickened to consistency of cream). Chill fish and
pour gelatin over fish until the platter is almost full.
Strain the remainder; put into a bowl and set all away
to cool and harden. When the fish is to be served, chop
the reserved jelly and spread over it, garnishing with
parsley and sauce.

   Modern Cooking Tip: Smaller farmed trout
commonly available can be substituted for 5-pound
trout, cooking 10 minutes for each inch of thickness of
the filet.

Sauce à la Diable

Makes about ⅔ cup.
3 hard-boiled eggs, chopped
¼ cup chopped onion
¼ cup chopped parsley
3 tablespoons olive oil
3 tablespoons French (Dijon) mustard
Salt to taste
1 tablespoon lemon peel (grated)

*At a formal World's Colum-
bian Exposition dinner,
thirty distinguished guests
engaged in pleasant banter,
including this joking query:
"Doesn't hors d'oeuvre mean
'out of a job?'"*

2 tablespoons vinegar (white wine)
1 teaspoon pepper
2 tablespoons lemon juice
¼ cup capers

Mix all ingredients well and serve in a gravy boat with trout in aspic.

Crab Flake Sublime

On preparing toast: "The object is to evaporate all moisture. Holding a slice over the fire to singe it does not do this. It only warms the moisture, makes the inside doughy and indigestible. The true way of preparing toast is to cut bread into slices a quarter-inch thick, trim crusts, put slices in a pan, place in a moderate, never hot, oven. Take out when a delicate brown and butter at once."

Makes 6 servings.
6 sliced fresh mushrooms
6 slices ham
1 pint (2 cups) crabmeat flakes
1 pint (2 cups) cream
Salt to taste
⅛ teaspoon cayenne pepper
2 egg yolks
2 tablespoons sherry
1 tablespoon butter
¼ cup cracker crumbs
Truffles for garnish (optional)
6 slices toast

Fry (sauté) mushrooms and ham until brown (in a deep-sided frying pan). Remove the ham, add crab flakes to the mushrooms, and pour in cream. Season with salt and cayenne pepper and let boil for 5 minutes. Beat the egg yolks with sherry, and with it thicken the mixture (stirring constantly). Pour all into (1-quart) casserole, sprinkle with some buttered cracker crumbs, and garnish with truffles. (Bake in a 325-degree oven for 10–15 minutes, until crumbs have browned.) Lay the slices of ham on toast (on individual plates), divide the crabmeat over same, and serve.

Modern Cooking Tip: Crackers can be crumbed in a blender or food processor. With an eye toward economy, the modern cook may wish to dispense with the truffle garnish.

Poached Salmon with Seafood Sauce

Makes 4 servings.
2 pounds fresh salmon filets
6 cups cold water
Salt to taste
1 sliced onion
½ glass (½ cup) white wine vinegar
8 peppercorns
2 cloves
2 parsley sprigs (about ¼ cup chopped plus parsley to garnish)

Place salmon in kettle. Cover all with cold water. Salt. Add onion, vinegar, peppercorns, cloves, parsley. Five minutes after coming to boil, salmon will be cooked (cook 10 minutes for every inch of thickness of filet). Remove (reserving stock for sauce). Drain well. Dress on hot dish, decorate with parsley greens. Serve with seafood sauce.

Seafood Sauce

Frank Family Recipe

Makes about 2 cups.
1 cup liquid in which salmon was cooked (or fish stock)
1½ teaspoons flour
4 egg yolks
¼ pound (½ cup) butter
2 tablespoons tarragon vinegar
1 tablespoon lemon juice
1 tablespoon Worcestershire sauce

After an 1896 dinner party given in honor of Robert Todd Lincoln at the Potter Palmer mansion, Mrs. Glessner described gilt and fine lace decoration, servants clad in liveries, and sherry that turned out to be whiskey. She observed, "The whole thing was costly and ostentatious. . . . We made up our minds that we like better our small unpreten-

tious dinners where people are brought together for the pleasure of meeting each other and not to fill a table or room which seats a certain number of people."

Paprika, salt, and pepper to taste
½ cup lobster, shrimp, and/or crabmeat (cooked and shredded)

(Over low flame in saucepan) thicken liquid in which salmon was cooked with flour and add other ingredients. If too thick, add more liquid at last minute, otherwise it will curdle. Mix lobster, salmon, and crabmeat with sauce and pour over salmon.

Codfish Soufflé

When Frances Glessner and her two children departed from Chicago to spend summers at the family's New Hampshire estate, Mrs. Glessner left the following elaborate instructions for the cook in her absence: "Mr. Glessner does not like fish, very thick soups, banana, cereals, currant short cake, lemon pie, tea, coffee, chocolate, drinks of any kind, sausage, honey, most sweets. Only occasionally bacon, ham, ice cream, salt fish."

Makes 4 servings.
2 tablespoons flour
2 tablespoons melted butter
Pinch of pepper
1½ cups milk
1 teaspoon onion juice
1 tablespoon finely chopped parsley
1 pound freshened (washed) salt codfish, picked into bits
3 eggs (separated)

In a skillet or saucepan, mix together flour and butter and add a pinch of pepper. (In skillet or saucepan), stir in milk and cook until boiling. Add onion juice, parsley, codfish, and the beaten egg yolks. Mix all together thoroughly, then fold in the whites of the eggs beaten dry. Bake in a buttered 9-inch casserole dish in a moderate oven (375 degrees) until firm in the center (30–40 minutes).

Modern Cooking Tip: Salt cod must be soaked for 48 hours in several changes of water in a glass, enamel, or stainless steel pan to freshen this tough fish for cooking. Almost any firm-fleshed whitefish such as halibut, sole, or flounder may be substituted for salt cod.

Baked Shad with Shad Roe Sauce

Makes 4 servings.

1 whole shad (scaled and slit)
1 cup dry bread crumbs
¼ pound (½ cup) butter (plus 1 tablespoon butter
for basting)
⅓ cup onion, chopped fine
1 tablespoon parsley, minced
1 tablespoon fresh or 1 teaspoon dried thyme
¼ cup tomatoes (canned, crushed or stewed)
3 tablespoons Worcestershire sauce (2
tablespoons reserved)
Salt and pepper to taste
1 tomato, sliced
1 tablespoon hot water
1 glass (1 cup) sherry
2 tablespoons lemon juice
Dash of hot sauce

The baking of the shad necessitates the cook's
remaining at home and being in her most amiable
mood, as basting is an essential. Make stuffing of
bread crumbs, butter, onion, parsley, thyme, canned
tomato, 1 tablespoon Worcestershire sauce, and salt
and pepper. Mix together and stuff lightly. Place shad
in baking pan. Top with slices of raw tomato, salt, and
pepper. (Bake in a 350-degree oven for 40–45
minutes.) Baste several times while baking with 1
tablespoon butter and a bit of hot water. Just before
done, pour over sherry, 2 tablespoons of
Worcestershire sauce, lemon juice, and hot sauce.
Serve with shad roe sauce.

Modern Cooking Tip: Have fishmonger scale and slit
the shad, leaving head and tail intact for an attractive
presentation.

Shad Roe Sauce

Makes about 2 cups.

Roe of 1 shad
1 tablespoon salt
6 cloves
2 bay leaves
1 bunch of thyme (about 1 cup fresh or ¼ cup dried)
1 teacup (½ cup) butter
Pinch of cayenne pepper
1 tablespoon tomato sauce
1 tablespoon lemon juice
1 glass (cup) sherry or Madeira

Prepare in chafing dish (or saucepan on stovetop) so you have ready when shad is sent up in dumb waiter. Roe should be parboiled in water (enough to cover) with salt, cloves, bay leaves, and thyme (for 12 minutes; drain). Remove roe skin. Pick it up with a silver fork and place in chafing dish (or saucepan) with butter and cayenne. When the butter is melted, stir in tomato sauce, lemon juice, and sherry or Madeira. Cook 5 minutes and serve.

Curry of Fish

Lilian Bell received an invitation to dine with Mr. and Mrs. Harry Hammer in the elegant Hotel Metropole; the purpose of the dinner was "to meet Miss Lilian Bell." Miss Bell replied:

My dear Mrs. Hammer,
So you have asked me to dine and to meet Lilian Bell!
The others may do as they like, but for my own part, I do not care to know her, and when I come, as I

Makes 4 servings.

1 teaspoon butter
1 tablespoon chopped onion
1 teaspoon curry powder
½ pint (1 cup) water or white stock (veal broth; see recipe, p. 48)
1 pound cold fish (2 cups, cooked and flaked)

Put into the chafing dish (or saucepan on stovetop) butter and onion and brown the latter. Add curry powder, water or broth, simmer 3 minutes, add cold fish, heat through and serve.

Modern Cooking Tip: This recipe is a quick way to spice up any leftover fish, and also works well from scratch using crabmeat.

Halibut à la Poulette with Yellow Sauce

Makes 4 servings.

4 halibut filets
¼ cup melted butter
Salt and pepper to taste
⅛ teaspoon onion juice
1 teaspoon lemon juice
¼ cup flour
Hard-boiled egg (sliced), lemon slices, and parsley for garnish

Dip (fillets) in butter, seasoned with salt, pepper, onion juice, and lemon juice. Roll and fasten with skewers. Dredge with flour (sprinkle to cover), place in small pan, and bake in hot oven (375 degrees) for 15 minutes. Arrange on platter, garnish with hard-boiled egg, lemon, and parsley. Serve with yellow sauce.

Yellow Sauce

Makes about 1½ cups.

1½ cups milk
1 slice onion
1 sprig parsley
1 blade mace (½ teaspoon)
1 small bay leaf
1½ tablespoons butter
1½ tablespoons flour
Yolks of 2 eggs
Salt and pepper to taste

strongly propose doing, pray see to it that we do *not* meet.

Should the time come when other people bore me to extinction, I may be obliged to console myself with her society. But until that unlooked-for time arrives, bid those to meet her who love her more than I do.

With very much love, believe me, dear Mrs. Hammer,
Yours most sincerely,
Lilian Bell

A delightful addition to the presentation of a Victorian table might be this method for serving garnishes in "tomato baskets," described as follows: "Select small, high tomatoes. Cut pulp away on each side at right angles . . . thus leaving a handle for basket. Make sure basket stands on stem end. Use to hold tartar sauce; serve with fish."

Scald milk with onion, parsley, mace, and a bit of bay leaf. Remove the seasonings (bay leaf and mace). Melt butter. Add flour (whisk until combined with butter but do not brown). Pour the scalded milk slowly on this (stirring constantly). Add (whisk in) egg yolks. Salt and pepper to taste.

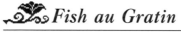 Broiled Mackerel

Broiled mackerel was a regular at breakfast on Prairie Avenue. But when Addie Hibbard discovered her fiancé was no mackerel man, she saw to it that he was served beefsteak, creamed potatoes, and waffles at their first breakfast together.

Allow 1 mackerel for every 2 people, adjust other proportions accordingly.

Makes 2 servings.
1 whole mackerel
2 teaspoons butter
Salt and pepper to taste

Cut off the head and tail, split down the back, extract the bones. Put on a gridiron and broil over or in front of a clear fire (brightly burning)—(broil for 4–5 minutes). Sprinkle a little pepper and salt over it before serving.

Modern Cooking Tip: Mackerel can be purchased filleted but will taste better if filleted again at least 1 minute.

Fish au Gratin

The Harvey children delighted in watching the live lobsters crawling on the kitchen floor, before they were boiled in the family's laundry tub.

Shortall Family Recipe

Makes 4 servings.
⅓ cup minced onion
1 tablespoon butter
1 tablespoon flour
1 cup white stock (veal broth; see recipe, p. 48)
1 gill (½ cup) pale sherry
6 chopped mushrooms
1 teaspoon chopped parsley

1 pound (2 cups) of any cooked whitefish
Flavored bread crumbs to cover
Parmesan cheese to garnish
2 tablespoons butter

Any good whitefish may be used. Bake or broil
previously. Fry (sauté) onion in butter, when brown,
stir in flour. To this add white stock, sherry,
mushrooms, parsley. Cut fish into small bits and lay
in gratin dishes. Pour sauce over, cover with fine
bread crumbs, sprinkle with a little Parmesan cheese
(to cover top). Dot with pieces of butter and bake (in a
350 degree oven for 15–20 minutes, or until bread
crumbs brown and liquid begins to bubble).

Fish Forcemeat

Makes about 2¾ cups.
12 ounces of raw whitefish (about 1½ cups,
filleted)
8 ounces (1 cup) bread crumbs
4 ounces (½ cup) butter
Yolks of 4 eggs
1 tablespoonful of chopped parsley
2 tablespoons lemon juice
Salt and pepper to taste
⅛ teaspoon nutmeg

Any other kind of (white-fleshed) fish will do if
whitefish is not at hand. See that it is free from bones
and skin, cut it up, and pound (puree) it in a bright
(nonaluminum) pan. Throw in all the other
ingredients, the butter not melted, and pound them
together till smooth. This delicate paste is useful in a
number of ways.

Modern Cooking Tip: Fish may be pureed in the
food processor, first by itself and then with other
ingredients added. The forcemeat can easily be made
into seafood sausages. Place mixture into a strip 1

*Mr. Wentworth Jerome
Field received an invitation
to dine with two ladies, to
which he replied to his hostess with sanctimonious deco-
rum, "Thanking you for
your wise dispensation of
pleasure."*

inch wide and 9 inches long at the top of a 10–12-inch-square piece of plastic wrap and roll up into sausage shape. Form into three 3-inch sausages and twist plastic between sausages and at ends. Place into simmering water to poach for about 10 minutes. Unwrap and serve.

The World's
Columbian
Exposition

The single event that crystallized the aspirations of a city on the move and its leading citizens was the dazzling World's Columbian Exposition of 1893. Following the success and pride of America's first great world's fair, the Phildelphia Centennial Exhibition of 1876 celebrating the founding of the United States, a number of individuals began proposing an idea for another fair: one that honored the four hundredth anniversary of Columbus's discovery of the New World and would highlight the achievements of the Americas. A senator from Illinois was persuaded to introduce a bill in Congress lending government support to such an exposition. It passed, and the race was on among bidding cities.

The ardor with which Chicago pursued the commission was best described during a meeting of the New York Chamber of Commerce: "When I meet a Chicagoan . . . whether his mission is for the welfare of my soul or my body, his first question is, 'What is your opinion of the world's fair location?' My hotel bill there had upon it 'The World's Fair in Chicago.' Upon a prescription I got for my cough, 'The World Fair.'. . . When I went to church, the lady who occupied the pew into which I was ushered handed me a prayer book upon which was pasted 'The World Fair in Chicago.'"

All suspense ended when Chicago offered to double the largest sum proposed for the funding of the exposition, and competitors retreated from the race. Planning began in earnest, but so grand were the designs for the fair that it soon became obvious that meeting the 1892 target date was beyond the ability of even the determined Chicagoans. Since the date of Columbus's sailing could not be changed, the committee instead held a dedication ceremony for the

15. Overview of the World's Columbian Exposition, showing the Manufactures and Fisheries buildings.

exposition in the city's Auditorium Hotel and Theatre on October 12, 1892.

Prairie Avenue patrons arrived at this gala in carriages marked with special badges that opened the way through the throngs pressed around the Auditorium Building. Inside the Adler and Sullivan masterpiece, Kinsley Catering Service presented a flower-adorned buffet table displaying a huge salmon surrounded by a selection of appetizers. In the words of a reporter covering the gala event, Christopher Columbus was that night "served hot, medium, cold, in ice cream and eloquence."

The fair was planned and executed by a stellar gathering of well-known architects, designers, and artists led by Daniel H. Burnham, a gathering proclaimed by sculptor Augustus Saint Gaudens "the greatest meeting of artists since the fifteenth century." The fair opened on May 1, 1893, an immense and well-planned gathering of gleaming white buildings, many of which were even electrified. Bertha Honoré Palmer, wife of Potter Palmer and arbiter of Chicago society, headed the "Board of Lady Managers" of the fair, which successfully promoted the creation of a Women's Building for the display of the artistic achievements of women. Her board even published their own cookbook, *Favorite Dishes—A Columbian Autograph Souvenir Cookery Book*, which boasted more than three hundred recipes contributed "specially by the Board of Lady Managers of the World's Columbian Exposition." Chicago Society prepared for the onslaught of visitors by redecorating their homes to impress and accommodate an overwhelming number of guests. George Pullman responded to the fever pitch of pride and patriotism generated by the fair by commissioning a statue commemorating the Fort Dearborn Massacre, which was placed by his house under the famous "massacre tree," where the infamous event was believed to have occurred.

Three hundred forty-two thousand people gathered to witness the opening of the great fair on May 1, 1893. From Mr. Higinbotham's private room, Mrs. Glessner watched the grand event: "President Cleveland opened the fair, the Statue of the Republic was unveiled, the fountains played, and flags from every pinnacle and turret were unfurled, the orchestra played 'America.' It was a grand and touching sight." More than 21 million visitors came to witness the shining "White City," as the fair was known, during its six months of existence.

The fair ended tragically, just hours before its scheduled closing,

16. Bertha Honoré (Mrs. Potter) Palmer, ca. 1905.

with the assassination of Chicago's mayor Carter Henry Harrison I at his home on October 28, 1893. Closing ceremonies were canceled, and flags were lowered to half-mast, thus bringing an end to one of the world's most spectacular and popular fairs. Many fragments of this event survive: smaller buildings, sculpture, and decorative details moved and reused in parks and private estates throughout the Midwest. The former Fine Arts Building from the fair now houses the Museum of Science and Industry, which, with the smaller-scale statue of the Republic from the fair, stands as testimony to this once magnificent event on Chicago's South Side.

17. The George Pullman drawing room, 1729 Prairie Avenue.

Poultry

ఙGalantinedeDende,Lucullus

Although few modern cooks would attempt the
Galantine de Dende, Lucullus (boned turkey),
described below, it offers a taste of the intricate
preparations that went into the dedication dinner for
the Columbian Exposition.

Take a hen turkey of 7 pounds, singe off the hair by
passing it over some lighted alcohol, cut off the head
and neck, make an incision through the back its
entire length, cut off the wings, and remove all the
bones of the turkey.

Take 3 pounds of chopped sausage meat, the half of
which place in the interior of your turkey, cover the
farce (the stuffing) with alternate strips of larding
pork, ½ inch wide, strips of cold ham, tongue, and
some truffles cut in pieces intermixed. Season with
pepper. Place on top of these the other half of your
sausage meat, which cover with another layer of
larding pork, ham, and truffles. Then draw the meat
at the sides to the center of the back of your turkey
and sew them together with a larding needle threaded
with fine twine. Place on top several slices of lemon,
from which you have removed the peel and seeds, and
wrap up your turkey very tightly in a cloth, which tie
firmly with a string, and put in a saucepan in which
you have put the bones of your turkey, a carrot, an
onion, a little thyme, 2 bay leaves, 2 cloves, 1 clove of

*The level of haute cuisine at
the Columbian Exposition
dedication ceremony was
such that it stumped report-
ers covering the event, who
could only describe the
menu as consisting of "won-
derful looking dishes with
strange sounding names."
Grappling with the "strange
sounds" of the menu in
readying it for the composi-
tors created a minor stir at
the newspapers.*

garlic, and enough consommé to cover the turkey.

Simmer gently for 3 hours, then remove the cloth. Clean it and again wrap the turkey in it as tightly as possible. Place it in a pan, put another pan on top, in which put a weight, so as to render the top of the turkey perfectly flat, and put on ice for a day. Skim off the grease from the liquid in which your turkey was cooked, strain, take of it 3 pints, which put on the fire with 3 ounces of gelatin and the juice of 2 lemons. Mix 4 whites of eggs with a glass of water, pour into your saucepan with the stock and gelatin, stir all well together, and when beginning to boil, remove to the back of the range to simmer gently for ½ hour. Strain through a flannel until perfectly clear, add a wineglass of sherry, put on the ice until cold, cut in pieces, which place on top around your turkey.

Roast Turkey with Bread Stuffing

This recipe uses a traditional crisping method in which the outside of the turkey is salted and sprinkled with flour. As the turkey begins to cook, the salt will pull out some of the juices, which will mix with the flour to create a crust, thereby trapping remaining juices and keeping the bird moist.

Makes 8–10 servings.
10-pound turkey
4 cups bread crumbs (dry)
Butter as large as an egg (¼ cup)
1 large white onion
1 teaspoon salt (for stuffing)
1 teaspoon pepper (for stuffing)
Additional salt and pepper to taste
2 tablespoons flour
1 coffee cup (1 cup) water

A turkey a year old is considered best. See that it is well cleansed and washed. Salt and pepper it inside (to

The great feasts of Thanksgiving and Christmas were always occasions for the gathering of clans on Prairie Avenue. At the Harveys there was always roast pig and two turkeys. Mrs. Harvey carved the pig, and Dr. Harvey the turkey. If the doctor thought the turkey was tough, he told the maid to "turn it around" their code for going to the kitchen for the second bird.

"The Christmas turkey should be cooped up and fed well some time before Christmas. Three days before it is slaughtered, it should have an English walnut forced down its throat three times a day, and a glass of sherry once a day. The meat will be deliciously tender, and have a fine nutty flavor."

taste). Take a loaf and a half of stale (or dried-out) bread and rub it quite fine with your hands (to make bread crumbs).

Have butter in your skillet, cut onion into; let it cook for a few minutes but not get brown. Then stir in your bread (crumbs), salt, pepper; let it get thoroughly heated. (Let cool and stuff and truss bird.) Put the turkey into a dripping pan; salt and pepper the outside (to taste) and sprinkle a little flour over it. Put water in the pan; baste very frequently; use a good moderate oven (325 degrees); roast about 3 hours, or 3½. Be sure to keep up an even fire.

Modern Cooking Tip: With current feeding methods, a turkey no longer need grow for a year to be a tender bird; 6 months or less is sufficient.

Roast Goose

Makes 4–6 servings.

8-pound goose
Salt and pepper to taste
½ teaspoon ground ginger

Salt the inside of the bird and stuff with apple or chestnut stuffing (see recipes, p. 86). Truss and prick the skin along the breast and around the legs. Roast in a moderate oven (375 degrees), uncovered on a rack (in a deep-sided roasting pan), basting every 15 minutes with drippings. When skin begins to brown, season with salt, pepper, and a few dashes of ground ginger. An 8-pound goose will require about 3½ hours for roasting.

Modern Cooking Tip: As most geese are not farm raised and leaner, they require less cooking time than was necessary at the turn of the century. An 8-pound goose should be roasted approximately 2½ hours, or until the juices run clear when the thickest part of the thigh is pricked with a fork.

"In selecting a goose or duck," advised a nineteenth-century culinary sage, "take hold of the toes and pull them apart. If the web separates easily, it is young; but if it requires any great amount of physical force to separate, lay it to one side . . . 'tis an old fowl, and you will reap no profit from its purchase unless you are keeping boarders."

 Apple Stuffing for Goose

Makes 3 cups.
½ **pound (about 1 cup) apple pulp**
2 **cups bread crumbs (dry)**
½ **teaspoon sage**
½ **cup finely chopped onion**
⅛ **teaspoon cayenne pepper**

Take the pulp of tart apples, which have been baked or scalded. Add bread crumbs, some powdered sage, a finely shredded onion and season well with cayenne pepper. Mix all ingredients together well.

Modern Cooking Tip: Bread crumbs can be fine or coarse, depending on the consistency desired for the stuffing. A cup of a natural, unsweetened applesauce can be substituted for the apple pulp.

Chestnut Stuffing for Goose

Makes 4 cups.
2½ **cups chestnut meat**
½ **cup light sweet cream**
1 **cup bread crumbs**
¼ **teaspoon pepper**
1 **teaspoon salt**

Boil the chestnuts and shell them; then blanch them and boil until soft; mash them fine and mix with a little sweet cream, some bread crumbs, pepper, and salt. Excellent for roast turkey.

Modern Cooking Tip: Chestnuts may be pureed in a food processor; if canned chestnuts are used, they do not need to be boiled and blanched first. Unsweetened canned chestnut puree may also be substituted.

Potato Stuffing for Goose

Makes 3 cups.

2 cups bread crumbs (dry)
1 cup broiled potatoes, grated
Butter the size of an egg (¼ cup)
½ teaspoon pepper
1 teaspoon salt
1 egg
1 teaspoon ground sage

Mix all ingredients thoroughly.

Quail on Fried Cornmeal Mush

Makes 4 servings.

8 quails
Salt and pepper to taste
¼ cup sweet butter (unsalted, at room temperature)
¼ cup lemon juice
¼ cup cream
½ cup sherry

Wipe the quail and split down the back. Salt and pepper them inside and out. Rub with sweet butter, lemon juice, and a touch of rich cream. Put them on a broiler (rack) in a hot oven (375 degrees for 15 minutes, or until juices run clear when pricked with a fork). Baste from time to time with sherry. Serve on fried cornmeal mush.

Fried Cornmeal Mush

Makes 1 loaf of fried cornmeal.

4 cups boiling water
1 cup cornmeal
1 teaspoon sugar

On April 10, 1893, world-famous pianist Ignace Paderewski visited Prairie Avenue to dine at the home of John and Frances Glessner. For this august guest, she staged an extensive meal of cream soup, fish, cucumbers and new potatoes, boiled chicken, peas, eggplant, asparagus with white sauce, tomato salad, crackers, ice cream, strawberries, cake oranges, coffee, candy, and grapes, followed by sherry and champagne. Following dinner, Paderewski matched his hostess's presentation with a performance upon her beloved Steinway piano.

Following the Fitch's elegant dinner for eighteen guests in their Michigan Avenue home, guests retired to the parlor for games. Mrs. Harold Hammer recalled winning a "pretty Royal Worcester looking tray and Harry took a gentleman's prize—a pearl paper knife."

1 teaspoon salt
¼ cup butter

Stir dry ingredients slowly into the boiling water. Boil 10 minutes, stirring often. Pour into a (8½-by-4½-by-2½-inch) loaf pan and chill thoroughly to harden. Cut into slices and sauté in butter in a heavy skillet until brown on both sides.

Potted Pigeon

Early settlers in the Prairie Avenue area lived a less refined life than their 1880s counterparts. Hardware merchant Henry Clarke and his wife, Caroline, filled their unfurnished front parlor with "half a dozen deer, hundreds of snipe, plover and quail, and dozens of prairie chickens and ducks" in the 1840s.

Makes 4 servings.

2 cups bread crumbs
5 tablespoons butter (3 tablespoons reserved)
¼ teaspoon salt (for stuffing)
⅛ teaspoon pepper (for stuffing)
Additional salt and pepper to taste
½ teaspoon summer savory
1 egg
4 pigeons
3 tablespoons flour (2 tablespoons reserved)

Make a stuffing of bread and (2 tablespoons of butter), seasoned with salt, pepper, and summer savory, worked together with an egg. When the birds are ready for cooking, put a ball of stuffing in each; sprinkle salt, pepper, and 1 tablespoon of flour over them and place them in a pot with the neck down, covering them with water (halfway up). Cover the pot and let them cook slowly (in 325-degree oven for 30–40 minutes). Watch them and turn them, if necessary. If they prove tough, they may require more water; if tender, you may have to take them up before the water is boiled down to make the gravy.

Put (reserved) butter and flour (whisked together until butter is absorbed) to the gravy (reduced to 2 cups) and lay the pigeons into it again (place in oven uncovered) that they may brown a little; when this is done, serve hot.

Pheasant Pie with Oysters

Makes 6–8 servings.

2⅓-pound pheasant (will yield about 1½ cups
boned and shredded cooked pheasant meat)
1 bay leaf
⅛ cup whole pepper
¼ cup chopped celery
4 tablespoons butter
2 tablespoons flour
½ cup of the water in which pheasant is cooked
½ cup milk
¼ teaspoon salt
¼ teaspoon pepper
¼ teaspoon nutmeg
2 9-inch piecrusts (see recipe, p. 157, or use
commercially prepared crusts)
12 raw (whole, shucked) oysters (about ½ pound)

Boil a pheasant till almost done; it will finish cooking
in the pie (braise in water to cover, seasoned with bay
leaf, pepper, and celery about 1½ hours, or until fork
tender). Make as much gravy as the size of the bird
will require (heat butter and flour for about 5
minutes, turn down flame, gradually add ½ cup of the
water in which pheasant was cooked and milk,
stirring until smooth); season (with salt, pepper, and
nutmeg) and thicken it (simmer for 5 minutes).

Make a good piecrust, and then put the pieces of
pheasant in. Scatter raw oysters among the pieces of
pheasant, pour over all enough gravy to fill the dish to
the depth of 1 inch, and cover it with crust, which
must be pressed against the edge so that it will
adhere. (Cut a ½-inch vent in the center of the pie.)
Let it bake for ½ hour (or until golden brown, in a
375-degree oven). After it is cooked, pour in remainder
of the gravy in the slit in the crust (if desired).

*When asked by a dear friend
why she had tacked the
French "RSVP" to the end
of an invitation in English,
Mrs. William Hibbard
quipped, "Oh! Those letters
stand for 'Remember Supper
Very Prompt.'"*

In June 1893 the Glessners visited the World's Columbian Exposition to "see the illumination" and dine with the fair's principal architect, Daniel Burnham. Accompanied by equally famed architects Mr. McKim and Mr. Mead in Burnham's launch, the group sailed around the lagoon twice, dined at the German village, toasted the evening, and sailed after dinner for the remainder of the evening. Mrs. Glessner recorded in her journal, "It was a night to remember."

 ## Roast Partridge

Harvey Family Recipe

Makes 6 servings.

3 partridges
7 tablespoons butter (3 tablespoons reserved)
1½ cups bread crumbs
3 tablespoons butter

Rightly, to look well, there should be at least (3 birds) in the dish. Pluck, singe, draw, and truss them. Roast them for about 20 minutes (in a 350-degree oven). Baste them with butter . . . (when done) place them in a dish together with bread crumbs, fried nicely brown (in reserved 3 tablespoons of butter) and arranged in small heaps.

In Prairie Avenue houses where abstinence was observed, the rituals of headier entertainment were sometimes honored in strange ways. Marion Rosenwald Ascoli recalled, for example, that in her father's house the Japanese butler poured into beautiful crystal wineglasses, from a bottle wrapped in a white napkin, the purest of unfermented grape juice. "I must say the idea of drinking grape juice with duck or beef sounds revolting now, but that's what we did."

Breast of Duck

Makes 4 servings.

4–8 duck breasts (butterflied)
1 tablespoon butter per duck breast
Salt and pepper to taste
Currant jelly as an accompaniment

Wild duck requires but a few moments cooking; and as only the breast is eaten, it is always advisable to cut this free from the bone. All that is necessary is to put a little butter in the chafing dish (or frying pan over a low flame) and when very hot, add the breast of duck. It is best to cook the meat plain, seasoned with pepper and salt only, and serve with currant jelly.

A teal breast duck, cook 2¾ minutes on each side; red head, 3 minutes; and canvas back, 3¼ minute on each side. These time allowances are for the finest birds obtainable, and cooked rare.

Modern Cooking Tip: The recommended serving portion for teal breast duck is 2 breasts per person.

For other varieties of duck, 1 per person is considered a generous portion, and a half a duck per person can suffice, depending on accompaniments.

Chicken Breasts with Poulette Sauce

Makes 6 servings.
3 whole chicken breasts (skinned and boned)
1 teaspoon salt
Chopped parsley for garnish

Remove the breasts from several chickens, cut them lengthwise, each giving 4 pieces. Simmer them in salted water (to cover) until tender (about 10–15 minutes). Make a poulette sauce and pour over the breasts piled on a dish. Sprinkle with parsley chopped very fine. Use a generous amount of sauce.

Poulette Sauce

Makes 3 cups.
Yolks of 4 eggs
1 cup cream
1 pint (2 cups) white sauce (see recipe, p. 127),
made with chicken or veal stock
1 tablespoon butter
2 tablespoons lemon juice
1 tablespoon chopped parsley
¼ teaspoon nutmeg

Take a pint of white sauce (and heat it.) Beat egg yolks with cream. Remove the sauce from the fire and add it slowly to the eggs and cream, stirring all the time. Put it again on the fire (over a low heat) a moment to thicken but do not let it boil, or it will curdle. Add butter slowly, a small piece at a time, the

Entertainments for the duke of Veragua, Spain's royal representative to the World's Columbian Exposition, were not to be compromised by a massive fire in the home of his hosts. Despite their missing roof and upper stories, a magnificent royal luncheon was held on a beautifully decorated table, as if nothing had happened, while water trickled down the walls into a tarpaulin suspended under the damaged dining room ceiling.

lemon juice, chopped parsley, and nutmeg. Serve at once. Do not put the sauce together until it is time to serve, as it is likely to curdle after the eggs and lemon juice are in. Stir constantly, and for a moment after removing from the fire. Also for sweetbreads and other entrées.

Creamed Chicken

Makes 4 servings.
1 pint (2 cups) cream
1 tablespoon flour
¼ cup milk
1 pint (2 cups) cold (cooked) chicken, cut into small pieces
1 cup mushrooms, cut into small pieces
Salt and pepper to taste
Few drops onion juice (to taste)
Chopped parsley for garnish

Heat cream in a chafing dish (or in a saucepan on the stovetop); add flour, stirred smooth in cold milk. When boiling hot, add the chicken and mushrooms; season with salt and pepper and onion juice. (Garnish with) parsley. Serve at once.

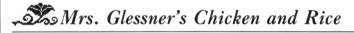Mrs. Glessner's Chicken and Rice

This recipe, collected by Mrs. Glessner in her travels, was found among her cookbooks, handwritten on stationery from the Hotel Touraine.

Makes 4–6 servings.
1 whole chicken (or 4 chicken breasts)
3 ounces of lean ham, cut in small dices (about ⅔ cup)
1 green pepper, chucked
1 onion, sliced
¼ cup olive oil
1 quart (4 cups) chicken stock
2 fresh tomatoes, peeled and sliced

1 cup rice (uncooked)
½ pound okra, sliced
Salt and pepper to taste

Take a whole chicken and take the skin off (then bone) and cut up in small square pieces. Add ham, green pepper, onion; fry all together in saucepan till onion comes golden color (sauté in olive oil for about 5 minutes). Then take very strong chicken stock; put all together with tomatoes, rice, okra. Simmer until rice is soft (about 15–20 minutes). Season to taste with salt and pepper.

18. Mary Dunham Staples (Mrs. John G.) Shortall, ca. 1885.

Meat and Specialty Dishes

❧ Young Roast Pig for Christmas

Makes 10–12 servings.

12–14-pound pig (milk-fed)
6–7 cups bread crumbs
3 eggs, well beaten
½ teacupful (¼ cup) butter
½ cup chopped onion
1 teaspoon powdered sage
¾ cup large raisins
Salt and pepper to taste
2 tablespoons water
1 tablespoon cream
2 tablespoons olive oil

Procure a fine young pig not more than 6 or 8 weeks old. See that the flesh is firm and pink and the eyes healthy and clear. Have it neatly dressed, leaving the head intact and the feet and tail au naturelle.

Prepare a dressing of bread crumbs, eggs well beaten, yolks and whites together, butter, onions, powdered sage, a handful of large raisins, and salt and pepper to suit the palate. Rub the inside of the pig with salt and pepper and lay along the backbone slices of salt pork, as the young meat needs the relish. Fill with the dressing, which is well mixed with water and a few spoonfuls of rich cream, and sew firmly together with a cord.

These festive serving suggestions accompanied this recipe: "When ready to a turn, place the pig on the platter on its knees; put on his back a little Chinese doll on a saddle of blue satin, with reins of smilax, and for a bit a kernel of popcorn; wire the cue of the doll so it will stand out straight, and you will be astonished at the rate of speed which his pigship is making across the table."

However, a sad footnote to this ritual. The Harvey children had a pet piglet at the family's summer home on Mackinac Island, which, unbeknownst to them, was being fattened for slaughter. The children remember with horror seeing their piglet, roasted, arrive at the Christmas table on the festive board garnished with mistletoe.

Put in a large baking pan (a minimum of 20 inches long), with the knees turned under and a small cob in the mouth to keep it open. Leave it to the mercies of a moderate oven (350 degrees) for 20 minutes, when the basting (with pan juices) must begin and be continued often at regular intervals until it is brown and tender (about 3 hours). For serving, place an apple in the pig's mouth and arrange on meat platter with the knees turned under on a bed of lettuce with other decorative garnishes.

Modern Cooking Tip: The addition of salt pork is not necessary to suit modern taste. Pig will brown nicely if rubbed with olive oil after trussing. At the risk of belaboring the obvious, readers are cautioned not to attempt this recipe before measuring their oven to ensure it is large enough.

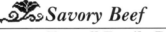 ## Savory Beef

Shortall Family Recipe

This recipe produces a traditional meatloaf, much like a paté in flavor and texture. Best the next day after flavors have had a chance to penetrate.

Makes 6–8 servings.
3½ pounds lean beef, chopped fine
Crumbs of 6 soda crackers, rolled fine as cracker dust (¾ cup cracker crumbs)
Butter the size of an egg (¼ cup), warmed a little but not melted
4 tablespoons light sweet cream
3 eggs, broken over the meat
1 tablespoon grated nutmeg
1 tablespoon marjoram
4 teaspoons salt
2½ teaspoons black pepper

The following Anderson family receipt is presented for the edification of those with a true passion for spiced beef and an infinite amount of patience: "Rub sugar well into 14 pounds of thick flank or rump of beef on all sides. Let stand in cool place for 12 hours. Then rub in salt, pepper, and allspice, all of which have been ground fine. Let stand another 12 hours. Then rub in salt. Turn daily in the liquor for two weeks. Dry thoroughly, cover with a coarse paste of flour and water. Put a little water in bottom of roasting pan and bake in a slow oven for four hours."

Knead it well with your hands, make it in 2 rolls, pressing very closely. (Mix all ingredients together well in a bowl, then shape into two loaves.) Put in a pan (deep-sided) and bake 1½ hours. When cold, slice.

Modern Cooking Tip: The suggested proportion for cracker crumbs takes into account that soda crackers of the turn of the century were much larger that today's. Modern taste dictates less salt, which can be quartered in this recipe without sacrificing flavor. Baked in a modern oven at 350 degrees, the beef should take only 1–1¼ hours to cook.

Syrian Lamb

Shortall Family Recipe

Makes 6 servings.

3 pounds shoulder of lamb
1 tablespoon butter
2 quarts (about 8 cups) string beans
1½ cups rice (uncooked)
2–3 onions, cut rather fine (1–1½ cups chopped onion)
1 quart (4 cups) tomatoes, roughly cut

Separate lamb from bones, cut into about 1-inch cubes, trim off some fat. Cook bones with meat for flavor but remove before serving. Sauté in deep kettle with a little butter about ½ hour. When brown, add string beans, rice, onion. When onions are brown, add tomatoes and water, if necessary, to cover meat well. Cover kettle, cook 20 to 30 minutes well, and another 30 minutes more slowly (over low flame).

After returning from a three-month tour of France and Italy, the Glessners dined at the home of Mr. and Mrs. Bartlett. To celebrate the journey, their hostess had created for each place setting "large dinner cards with an ocean scene painted in watercolors. John's was of New York harbor and the ship coming in, mine of the ship on the broad ocean—all with a large bow of sea green ribbon with name, date, and Mrs. B's monogram." Young May Bartlett then recited a poem, "bringing in every incident of our trip abroad which I had told," which had been composed by their host, Mr. Bartlett.

Mutton Chops

Glessner Family Recipe

Rib chops (1 inch thick and trimmed)
Cold vinegar
1 egg
Bread crumbs (one cup for 4–5 chops)
Pepper (½–¾ teaspoon)
Salt (½–⅗ teaspoon)
Nutmeg (½–¾ teaspoon)

Combine bread crumbs, pepper, salt, and nutmeg and put aside. Put vinegar into separate bowl. Beat egg and place in another bowl. Using the bone as a handle, dip chops thoroughly into vinegar, then into the beaten egg, followed by the bread crumb mixture. Then brown chops slowly in hot lard, about 10–15 minutes on each side on medium heat.

Modern Cooking Tip: Lard can be replaced with butter, Crisco, or vegetable oil in this recipe. Use about ½–¾ teaspoon of each salt, pepper, and nutmeg, to season to taste.

Meatballs

Rosenwald Family Recipe

Makes 2–4 servings.
1 pound ground sirloin steak
2 tablespoons cream
2 tablespoons butter, melted
Salt, pepper, and seasoning to taste

To a mixing bowl of ground sirloin steak, add cream a drop at a time, stirring constantly. When the mixture is like limp dough, shape patties 4 inches across and about 1 inch high. Cook in melted butter on top of the stove. Flip them quickly at first to seal in the juices

The Rosenwald daughters remembered their mother, then ill, sitting up in bed in a frilly bedjacket with a large mixing bowl of ground sirloin in her lap. She kept stirring while a maid, in a cap and apron, added one drop of cream at a time.

and then cook until both sides are brown and the inside is rare (about 2 minutes per side).

Chicken Livers and Chestnuts

Makes 2–4 servings.
1 pound chicken livers
¼ cup olive oil
1 pint (2 cups) chestnut meat
1 tablespoon flour
2 tablespoons butter
Approximately ½ cup hot water
Salt and pepper to taste.

Drain and fry (sauté) chicken livers in olive oil (only to brown). Shell and boil chestnuts until tender (then drain) and put them through a meat chopper. Cover the bottom of the casserole with a layer of livers, then a layer of chestnuts, alternating until all are used. Rub together flour and butter (and spread over top), add enough hot water to cover the mixture, salt and pepper to taste. Cover and bake (in a 350-degree oven) for 20 minutes.

Modern Cooking Tip: Chestnuts may be pureed in a food processor. If canned chestnuts are used, they do not need to be boiled first. Canned chestnut puree may also be substituted.

Corn Beef Hash

Makes 4 servings.
1 cup butter
2 cups water
4 cups cooked, finely chopped corn beef
2⅔ cups cold, finely chopped boiled potatoes
12 drops hot sauce
Salt and pepper to taste

Charles Hutchinson was known on Prairie Avenue for his Sunday morning breakfast, featuring corn beef hash and all the trimmings. Afterward, the Eternal Improver, as he was known to his wife, would lead his nieces in wild romps all over the house. Then he'd whoop down-stairs, bounce onto the piano seat, and play "Onward Christian Soldiers."

A private party held in the Old Vienna pavilion of the World's Columbian Exposition treated visitors to lively bands and singing in the beer garden, which lasted until midnight.

Melt the butter in the water, add the other ingredients, cook until thoroughly heated through (about 5 minutes), then put into a baking pan and place in the oven until brown on top (375 degrees for 10–15 minutes). Serve with white sauce if preferred (see recipe, p. 127).

Kidneys with Potatoes

Makes 4–6 servings.
4 lamb or veal kidneys
1 scant tablespoon butter
3 medium-size potatoes, peeled and diced
1 tablespoon celery
½ pint (1 cup) brown gravy
2 cups sliced mushrooms
¼ teaspoon salt
⅛ teaspoon pepper
1 tablespoon mushroom catsup (see recipe, p. 133)

Scald and skin the kidneys and quarter them. Put butter into the chafing dish (or into a saucepan on the stovetop), when quite hot put in the potatoes, stir to prevent sticking to the dish. Add the celery, then the kidneys and good rich brown gravy. If a few mushrooms are in the house, add them. Season with salt, pepper, and mushroom catsup. Cover and simmer 6 minutes and serve. The heat is so intense that the potatoes, cut small, cook in a few minutes.

Modern Cooking Tip: Whereas at the turn of the century, kidneys came encased in fat, they are now sold only skinned. To scaled kidneys: In a 5-quart or larger kettle, boil water with ¼ teaspoon salt added. Drop kidneys into boiling water until they turn white (20–30 seconds), remove immediately, and pull off skins and excess fat.

Sweetbreads

Makes 2–4 servings.
1 pair sweetbreads
¼ cups boiling water
½ teaspoon salt
1 tablespoon lemon juice
Salt, pepper, and paprika to taste
2–3 tablespoons butter

Put sweetbreads in cold water to cover (soak for 1 hour); remove pipes and membranes. Cook in boiling salted water with lemon juice, 20 minutes, and plunge into cold water to harden. Season with salt, pepper, and paprika. Fry (sauté) in butter in skillet. When brown, add water (about ¼ cup) to fat in skillet, cover, and let steam until served. This softens them perfectly. Frying and steaming together take about 20 minutes.

This recipe attests not only to the popularity of sweetbreads on Prairie Avenue but also to the fact that there was considerable recipe swapping done on the street. It comes form Mrs. Shortall's handwritten kitchen notes and credits the recipe to her neighbor, Mrs. Harvey.

Risotto

Shortall Family Recipe

Makes 4 servings.
4 tablespoons bacon, fat ham, or salt pork
½ cup onion, chopped
1½ cup canned tomatoes, broken up, with juice
2 tablespoons butter
1½ cup any meat, cooked or uncooked
1 cup hot water (¾ cup reserved)
1 cup uncooked rice
Grated cheese to garnish

Chop a little fat ham, salt pork, or bacon with onion. Brown in frying pan. Boil tomatoes and strain into above. Add a piece of butter. Chop any meat that you have cooked or uncooked, put into the tomato, add a little (¼ cup) hot water, and cook a few minutes, longer if using uncooked meat.

Wash rice and turn it, uncooked, into frying pan, mix well with meat, add a few spoonfuls (¾ cup) hot water and from time to time stir and add water (check after 10 minutes and add more water if needed). Add grated cheese at the last or pass separately to be put on at the table.

Modern Cooking Tip: Use canned, not fresh, tomatoes, which better emulate the consistency of the home-canned tomatoes that would have been used by cooks of the day. The best results are achieved with the use of a smoky flavored meat such as ham or smoked turkey. Risotto will be cooked al dente in 20 minutes after the addition of the rice.

 *Risotto*

Glessner Family Recipe

1 ounce of butter
½ pound rice (well picked, but not washed)
Pepper
Salt
Half an onion, chopped
1 pint basic meat gravy (flour, milk, and meat drippings blended and heated to taste)
Grated cheese

Heat butter in frying pan until light brown. Add rice and season with pepper, salt, and a little chopped onion. Let cook about 5 minutes. Then add meat gravy and cook uncovered until tender, about 15–20 minutes. Serve with grated cheese. Makes about 6 servings.

Modern Cooking Tip: Long grain wild rice works well with this recipe. A commercial gravy package mixed according to directions can be substituted for gravy if desired.

🍂 Pig's Feet à la S. Menehould

Makes 2–4 servings.
1 pound cooked and pickled pig's feet, boned
3 eggs
1½ cups bread crumbs
1½ cup vegetable oil
Parsley to garnish
Tartar sauce as an accompaniment

Egg and bread crumb pig's feet and fry (in oil, for about 5 minutes). Serve on a napkin with crisp parsley and pass with tartar sauce.

Modern Cooking Tip: To cook and pickle pig's feet; In a stock pot, put 8 cups water, 2 large carrots, peeled, 1 extra large white Spanish onion, peeled, with 2 cloves stuck in it, and ¼ teaspoon each of whole peppercorns and whole allspice, smashed. Bring to a boil and let cook for 10 minutes. Add 1 teaspoon each of thyme and salt, 1–2 sprigs parsley, and 1 bay leaf, along with 4 pig's feet, wrapped individually in cheesecloth. Simmer for 4 hours, then let cool, and carefully unwrap pig's feet.

Place pig's feet in a deep container. In skillet, put 1 cup vegetable oil, 2 cups white wine vinegar, 2 sliced onions, 4 teaspoons dried tarragon, 1 teaspoon minced garlic, and ¼ teaspoon each of salt and pepper. Heat over a medium flame until steaming (do not bring to a full boil). Pour mixture over pig's feet to cover. Let cool and refrigerate for 1½–2 days. Then remove bones and prepare according to cooking directions above.

🍂 Golden Birck (Welsh Rarebit)

Makes 4 servings.
1 pint ale
1 pound cheese (cheddar), cut into dice
1 tablespoon cream

Pig's feet meant many things to many people: In Chicago's Irish neighborhood of Bridgeport they were known as "Irish Quail"; to Mrs. Meeker of Prairie Avenue, they were "a gelatinous mess"; but her son, Arthur, considered them such a delicacy that he often inveigled their Irish cook to make quantities of them for friends at the Chicago Club. The final word on pig's feet comes from Mrs. Glessner's Christmas alphabet;

E is for eat
A very nice treat
Is the nice tender meat
Of well done pig's feet
This can't be beat.

1 saltspoon (¼ teaspoon) dry mustard
1 saltspoon (¼ teaspoon) salt
Pinch of cayenne pepper
4 slices toast
4 poached eggs

Pour into saucepan of your chafing dish and set directly over the blaze (or put in a saucepan on the stovetop) a pint of good ale. When it boils, stir in cheese. As it melts, add cream, dry mustard, and salt, with a generous pinch of cayenne. Stir until the whole mixture is hot and ladle out upon hot toast or toasted crackers. Lay a poached egg on each serving.

 ## Venison Steak

Makes 4 servings.
1½-inch-thick venison steak (about 24 ounces) or 4 individual steaks (5–6 ounces each)
2 tablespoons butter
Salt and pepper to taste
2 gills (1 cup) port wine
1 tablespoon pure red currant jelly

Lay steak in the chafing dish (or frying pan) in which butter has been melted. Season with pepper and salt. Add port wine and red currant jelly. Cook until one side is done, then turn, and cook the other side. The degree of cooking must depend upon your own taste.

Modern Cooking Tip: Venison steak is best cooked 3–4 minutes per side to medium doneness, or slightly pink in the center.

Christmas of 1888 was a festive time at Glessner House. Holly decorated all the doorways, and twenty-one stockings were hung for children and servants. Mrs. Glessner had concocted her usual Christmas pie centerpieces, a pie tin chock full of little presents all buried in sand, and trimmed with a bouquet of flowers. For Christmas dinner, she cooked venison in a chafing dish at the dinner table.

Tamale Pie

Glessner Family Recipe

2 or 3 slices bacon cut fine
1 medium-size onion
2 tablespoons chopped parsley
1 green sweet pepper cut fine
1 pound ground beef and pork (or beef alone)
1 can tomatoes (14½ ounce can, peeled and chopped)
1 small can ripe seeded olives (3¼ ounce can, sliced in half and drained)
Salt
Pepper
1 teaspoon chili powder
½ pound cheese, if liked (yellow)
1 cup cornmeal

Cook chopped bacon and onion together. Add green pepper and parsley and cook till tender but do not brown, add meat. Stir and when meat begins to brown, add tomatoes, olives, and all seasonings except chili powder. When mixture boils, add cornmeal (mixed with enough cold water to dampen), chili powder, and cheese. Cook in large stockpot until thick mush and turn into greased baking dish and bake at 350 degrees for 45 minutes.

Modern Cooking Tip: Add more chili powder for a spicier dish.

A surprised George Glessner family found themselves traveling to Mexico City in 1921 amidst a revolution. Alice Hamlin Glessner recorded their reactions to this adventure: "Of course this startled us and Frances said she hoped we would be attacked, and I said I hoped we would not, and Mr. Glessner said he did not care as this same Washington man reminded him that we had left prohibition behind and that Orizaba beer was very good. This reconciled Mr. Glessner to anything Mexican."

19. Glessner House butler's pantry.

Servants

In the summer of 1892, John Shortall sent a thank-you note to Mrs. Glessner, then vacationing in the East. "Well, a bright, happy summer to you all," he wrote. "Plenty to eat, ravenous appetites, and a faithful cook to you! Can I pray better for you?"

Prayers were not uncalled for. As the size of homes increased, so did the number of servants required to maintain them. Society on Prairie Avenue had become more formal, and servants became an indispensable part of everyday life. The "hired girl" of earlier days had been replaced by a large team of live-in staff, each with specific duties often spelled out in books on household management.

Most large Prairie Avenue households had a housekeeper or butler, cook, laundress, houseman, a number of maids, nursemaids or governesses to care for children, coachman, footmen, and stable servants. The Glessner family even had a servant whose task was to keep the fires stoked and burning each day in the ten fireplaces of their winter residence on Prairie Avenue. Among the hierarchy of servants, household staff had greater prestige than stable servants, with the housekeeper or butler holding authority over household staff, and the coachman over stable servants. There seemed, in the eyes of one Prairie Avenue granddaughter, a constant procession of carriages taking ladies downtown to the employment offices and a never-ending pool of hopeful employees.

Large households became major employers and the ranks of servants required to maintain them were often filled with young, unmarried immigrants. Household domestic positions were largely held by women, and stable positions by men. Such work provided security, safety, and an average annual salary of $350 to $1,000; however, the trade-offs were dear. Servants had little privacy, worked 14–17-hour

20. Servant girls: *left*, Agnes McArthur and, *right*, Sophie Allard illicitly wearing Mrs. Glessner's dresses, at the family's summer estate, "The Rocks," in New Hampshire, ca. 1925. These dresses are now preserved in the collection of the Chicago Historical Society.

days, were on call 24 hours a day, were allowed only one afternoon or evening off each week and an occasional Sunday if the work was done. Employers could impose moral codes on their staff, such as required dress and hours of return on days off. In return, servants were expected to be silent and deferential.

The responsibilities of the housekeeper in many of the mansions were considerable, including hiring other servants as necessary, opening and closing the family houses, buying equipment and linens, reading to youngsters, ordering clothes, and taking children to dancing school and on trips. Cooks had to prepare the "first" table, while the kitchen maid readied the "second" table at which staff ate lunch at midday (excluding, of course, governesses and nurses, who dined on trays in their rooms or at the children's table). Because staffs were large, names could become a problem: at the Meekers there were Mary Keyes, the cook; Mary O'Hara, the waitress; Mary McKee, the laundress; and the Mary who was renamed Minnie, because with the birth of Mary Meeker, five Marys were just too many.

Few households were as large as the Marshall Fields', and Mrs. Field was reputed to have on staff "a representative from nearly every civilized nation of the globe." There were the French cook, the German maid, the English butler, the Norwegian footman, and an assortment of governesses, coachmen, kitchen help, seamstresses, and cleaning women. There was reportedly even an almoner, hired to make rounds of the city in search of the poor deserving of Mrs. Field's benefactions. Despite the numbers, Mrs. Glessner recorded in her diary that when Marshall Field, Jr., was married in October 1890, Mrs. Field asked if she might borrow the Glessners' butler rather than risk hiring a stranger. It was not an uncommon request, and guests often encountered trusted and capable servants from other Prairie Avenue households at a neighbor's social event.

Reputedly the best manager of servants on Prairie Avenue was Mrs. George Pullman, who was said to keep accounts and audit bills with a cultivated degree of business acumen. The most famous of the Pullman staff was butler Alexandre Testault, who had literally been captured from friends in New York. Dubbed "the prince of butlers" by the *Chicago Evening Post*, the debonair Testault became such a personage in Chicago that Robert Lincoln and Benjamin Harrison, among others, were reported to have been "proud to exchange witticisms with him."

In the Glessner household, servants were invited to watch the

21. Glessner House courtyard, ca. 1888, showing servant Violette E. Scharff petting the Glessner's dog, Hero.

lighting of the tree each Christmas with the family. The Glessners gave each servant a Christmas gift—in 1894 they were given an extra month's wages. On occasion the servants reciprocated: Frances Glessner recorded the following occurrence on their twentieth wedding anniversary in 1895. "Frederick (the butler) came in and in a graceful way asked me to accept two beautiful gravy ladles from the servants. With the spoons came a card 'with the best wishes of the servants' followed by their names arranged according to the length of time they have been with us. These gifts were all in the most perfect taste and touched us deeply. After dinner John called them in and thanked them for us both."

A number of changes in the first three decades of the twentieth century eventually reduced the servant population, ultimately threatening the continued existence of large, grand households. The stigma attached to domestic work coupled with the advent of labor-saving devices encouraged those in domestic positions to seek other options. Shifting priorities within the household prompted middle- and upper-class women to become more involved in operating the household and raising children. These changing attitudes and the decreasing number of servants available to work in large homes threatened the viability of running such households. By the end of the Great Depression many communities of grand homes such as Prairie Avenue stood vacant and derelict.

The difficulties of keeping a household running smoothly can be gleaned from entries made in Mrs. Glessner's diary during 1891: "I dismissed one cook on Monday; another one came to take her place, but number two dismissed this place next day on account of the gas range. Number three came in on Wednesday and walked out at once . . . Dora came today. She is very green looking and loud. I had to tell her she must not be heard in the house, both voice and shoes must be quiet . . . Mary the cook, boiling with rage because I ordered wine left from dinner poured into the cooking sherry."

In the Shortall residence, where notes in Mrs. Shortall's cookbooks record that menus for family and servants both averaged sixty-five cents a person per day, the following quiz was devised to help screen prospective kitchen staff:

1. What do you like best for deep frying, for fishballs or potatoes?
2. For frying in the pan, like fritters?
3. Did you do our tomatoes on toast in oven or broiler? Butter on

both sides of bread, as the recipe calls for? Bits of butter on tomatoes?

4. Does it help steer's liver to soak it in milk or did you give up doing that?
5. Did you make our creamed potatoes of raw or cooked potatoes?
6. How thick did you cut eggplant for frying?
7. How big did you cut piece of meat for Scotch broth?
8. What heat of oven for popovers?
9. How thick a batter did you make for our apple fritters? Please give recipe.

Side Dishes and Salads

Stuffed Onions

Makes 2 servings (easily doubled to serve 4).

1 large Spanish onion
½ cup cooked peas
Salt and pepper to taste
1 cup cooked mashed potatoes
1 hard-boiled egg (optional)

Cut a big Spanish onion in two (crosswise) and steam (in a vegetable steamer over boiling water for about 10 minutes, or until fork tender). Take out centers. Fill the halves with delicately seasoned peas; set the whole on a little bed of mashed potatoes and set in oven to brown (under broiler 2–3 minutes, watching carefully). Meanwhile, you will have chopped fine the centers of the onion and added to the minced centers a hard-boiled egg chopped fine, a filling for sandwiches.

Parsnip Fritters

Makes about 6 servings.

2 cups dry, mashed parsnips
Butter the size of an egg (¼ cup)
2 tablespoons of flour
2 eggs
1 teaspoon pepper

By the turn of the century, Chicago's South Water Street Market had become a great food center. "Imagine a little runway only five blocks long . . . its narrow streets packed and jammed with 10,000 wagons a day," reads an account of the period. "Fill one four-storied building to the roof with limburger cheese; pack the warehouse next door with Spanish and Bermuda onion, crowd the cellars and under ground caves with ripening bananas and pineapples, festoon the fronts with strings of jack rabbits, opossums, squirrels . . . then you get an idea of South Water Street on a busy day."

22. Theodore Thomas and his wife, Rose Fay Thomas, ca. 1900.

1 teaspoon salt
2 cups lard (vegetable shortening)

Stir all ingredients (except lard) together. Have a saucepan (heavy saucepan or frying pan) or lard hot enough to hiss when a drop of water touches it. Dip a spoon in (the parsnip mixture) and then shape a fritter with it, drop in, and fry light brown (takes about 10 minutes). Serve either with gravy or as an accompaniment to some kind of meat.

Modern Cooking Tip: Vegetable shortening may be substituted for lard.

Tomato Pie

4 cups ripe tomatoes (Italian tomatoes)
1 9-inch pie shell (see recipe, p. 157, or use commercially prepared shell)
2 tablespoons sugar
2 tablespoons butter, melted
4 tablespoons flour

Peel and slice thin, like apples, the ripe tomatoes (scrape out the juicy part around the seeds). Sprinkle flour (2 tablespoons) in bottom of partially baked pie shell and layer tomatoes in shell with flour (1 tablespoon) sprinkled in between each layer. Melt butter and mix sugar into it, drizzle over pie. Sprinkle flour (1 tablespoon) lightly over top, making sure it is moistened by tomato juice or butter. (Bake in a 350-degree oven for 35 minutes.)

Modern Cooking Tip: The use of denser, less juicy Italian tomatoes is essential to prevent a very runny pie. For additional flavoring, sprinkle basil or dill into tomato mixture and grate cheese on top.

Lydia (Mrs. William Gold) Hibbard's Sunday dinner guests frequently included a minister and his wife, both deaf-mutes. At each place at table were placed a pad with pencil so that all of the guests could converse.

Sir Henry Wood, British Commissioner to the World's Columbian Exposition, came to Chicago in 1893 to visit the grand event. Upon hearing that the Women's Building was the most substantial building of the fair and had been finished ahead of the other buildings, Sir Henry replied in amazement, "How did they do it? How did they do it? Did they crochet it?"

Green Corn Pudding

Harvey Family Recipe

Makes 10 servings.

12 large ears of sweet corn nicely grated (6 cups grated corn)
1½ pints sweet milk (3 cups whole milk)
4 eggs, beaten
2 tablespoons butter
½ teaspoon salt
1 cup sugar

Bake slowly 2 hours. To be eaten without sauce.

Modern Cooking Tip: The missing steps in preparation of this recipe are as follows: Mix all ingredients well and pour into buttered 3-quart mold. Place in a pan filled halfway up the side of the mold with warm water. Bake the pudding at 350 degrees for 2–2½ hours, or until a knife inserted in the center comes out clean. Puree the mixture in a blender if you prefer a smooth-textured pudding.

Broiled Mushrooms on Toast

Makes 1 dozen mushrooms.

1 dozen large white mushrooms
1 dozen toast rounds
3 tablespoons butter, cut into 12 thin slices
Salt and pepper to taste
Fried parsley for garnish

Trim off stalks of mushrooms, peel, score across the top. Place on a gridiron and grill over a slow fire (or in the broiler, watching carefully), turning them when done on one side (takes 2–3 minutes per side). Cut some slices of bread, trim off crusts, and toast them nicely on both sides. Cut some rounds out of toast the same size as mushrooms, butter them, and place a mushroom on each. Put a lump of butter in each mushroom and sprinkle over salt and pepper. Spread a fancy-edged paper over a hot dish, arrange the toasts neatly on it, garnish with fried parsley, and serve at once.

Stuffed Cucumbers

Makes 2 servings (easily doubled to serve 4).

1 large cucumber
½ cup fish forcemeat
6 slices bacon (3 slices reserved)
8–10 cups white stock (see recipe, p. 48)
1½ tablespoon flour
3 tablespoons butter

Peel a large cucumber. Remove narrow piece from inside. (Cut slice off top sufficient to allow for stuffing cucumber.) Scoop out seeds with a teaspoon. Fill cavity with forcemeat of lobster or salmon. Replace the piece and bind it round with thread. Line bottom of a saucepan with (3) slices of bacon. Put cucumber upon it and then (reserved) slices of bacon over it. Cover whole with seasoned stock. Simmer gently until cucumber is cooked (about 20 minutes). For gravy (remove bacon, reduce stock to 1½ cups and), thicken with a little flour and butter. Serve hot.

Modern Cooking Tip: The whitefish forcemeat recipe on page 00 can be used as is for the cucumber stuffing or easily adapted for preparation of lobster or salmon forcemeat. The substitution of a zucchini for the cucumber will produce a similar taste with firmer consistency.

At the sixth annual reunion of the Pioneers of Chicago on May 25, 1895, members reenacted pioneer days, playing the roles of "early old" settlers, country boys, mayors and officials, magistrates and doctors, real estate men, lumbermen, and railroad engineers invited to a dinner of little neck clams, consommé with olives and radishes, boiled salmon with sliced cucumbers and hollandaise potatoes, fillet of beef with mushrooms, potato croquettes, and green peas, followed by orange sherbet, lettuce and tomato mayonnaise, and dessert of neapolitan ice cream, assorted cakes, strawberries, coffee, and tea.

A rice recipe from an island cookbook on the period: "Wash him (rice) well; wash in cold water; the rice flour make him stick. Water boil all ready very fast. Throw him in; rice can't burn, water shake him too much; boil half and hour. Rub rice in thumb and finger. If all rub away, him quite done. Put rice in colander; hot water run away; pour cup of cold water on him, put back rice in saucepan, keep him covered near the fire. When rice all ready, eat him up."

The Meeker butler and the second man, in addition to their formal duties, played squash with the head of the household "so vigorously that he wrecked his arches." He also wrecked his wife's composure, when she discovered that he had pressed her china into service for the match.

Turkish Pilaf

Makes 4–6 servings.

1 cup tomatoes, stewed and pureed
1 cup of stock, seasoned with ¼ teaspoon salt, ⅛ teaspoon pepper, and 2 tablespoons minced onion
1 cup rice (uncooked)
½ cup butter

When boiling (tomatoes and stock), add rice. Stir lightly with a fork, then add butter, set on the back of the stove (or on low heat) or in a double boiler, and steam for 20 minutes (simmer until water is nearly absorbed). Remove the cover, stir in lightly, cover with a towel, and let steam escape. Serve as a vegetable.

Asparagus

Makes 4 servings.

2 dozen asparagus stalks
2 teaspoons salt
4 slices toast
2 tablespoons melted butter

Scrape stalks clean and throw into cold springwater. Tie in bunches (with string, about a dozen per bunch), cut root ends even, and place in bundles in muslin (cheesecloth, optional) to preserve tops. Have a wide stewpan of springwater salted. When water boils, lay in spears and boil quickly 10 minutes, or until tender. Have a slice or loaf nicely toasted, cut in square pieces, and dip them in asparagus water and put them in serving dish. Lay asparagus on toast and serve with melted butter in a tureen.

Modern Cooking Tip: With advance filtration, you need not set out in search of the local spring; asparagus will do fine boiled in tap water.

Creamed Potatoes

Makes 4 servings.

2 cups cold boiled potatoes, sliced ⅛ inch thick
1½–2 cups cream
1 tablespoon butter
½ teaspoon salt
Dash of pepper
1 teaspoon finely chopped parsley

Put potatoes in a saucepan with enough cream to cover them and cook until the potatoes have absorbed nearly all the cream; then add butter, salt, pepper, and, just before serving, parsley.

Sweet Potato Croquettes

Makes 10–12 croquettes.

1 quart (4 cups) mashed potatoes
½ cup boiled milk
¼ cup butter
Salt to taste
2 eggs, beaten lightly
1 cup cracker crumbs
2 cups vegetable oil

(Mix sweet potatoes, milk, butter, and salt together well and form 1½–2-inch balls.) Dip in crumbs, then in eggs, then in crumbs and fry as doughnuts (deep fry in vegetable oil in a heavy skillet for 3–5 minutes, or until golden).

Potato Salad

Glessner Family Recipe

A little butter (1 tablespoon)
Very little onion cut thin (1 cup)
½ cup vinegar

Bemoaning that not one housekeeper out of ten knows how to boil potatoes properly, the kitchen notes of one Prairie Avenue household recommend this Irish method: "Clean and wash the potatoes and leave the skin on; then bring the water to a boil and throw them in. As soon as boiled soft enough for a fork to be easily thrust through them, dash some cold water into the pot, let the potatoes remain 2 minutes, and then pour off the water. This done, half remove the pot lid, and let the potatoes remain over a slow fire till the steam is evaporated; then peel and set them on the table in an open dish. Potatoes of a good kind, thus baked, will always be sweet, dry and mealy. A covered dish is bad for potatoes, as it keeps the steam in and makes them soft and watery."

Residents on Prairie Avenue often gathered for informal evenings of cardplaying, which might include such refreshments as sherry, biscuits, claret cup, and small cakes. Following such an evening, Mrs. Glessner recorded treats of salad, rolls, coffee, chocolate cake, and claret cup. Mr. Glessner was presented with the booby prize: a copy of the book What I Know about Euchre. *Behind its handsomely decorated cover, all the pages were blank.*

Theodore Thomas, founding conductor of the Chicago Symphony Orchestra, had a particular eating regimen on concert nights, as indicated by his wife's reply to an invitation to dine at an evening party held at the home of John and Frances Glessner: "I hope you will not think me rude for asking you to provide for my husband a bit of meat and some brut champagne. He eats no dinner before a concert and is nearly famished by the time it is over, and dainty little dishes are too insubstantial and too rich unless he has a bite of something plain first." Upon arrival at Glessner House, the maestro was spirited off to the dining room for, we are told, "a nice hot supper of roast beef, champagne, rye bread, and asparagus salad."

Salt and pepper (½ teaspoon each, or to taste)
Boiled potatoes, sliced thin
1 tablespoon oil

Put a little butter in a spider (frying pan) with a very little onion (about 1 tablespoon). Stew in butter until cooked tender. Add vinegar and salt and pepper to taste. Place potatoes in layers with very thin slices with the rest of the onion between. Broil until top is golden brown, about 15–20 minutes, and remove from oven. Beat boiling butter and vinegar mixture into the oil, pour hot over the sliced potatoes.

Asparagus Salad

Makes 4 servings.
2 cups cold cooked asparagus tips
2 cups cooked crawfish tails or shrimp
¼ teaspoon salt
⅛ teaspoon pepper
Yolks of 6 hard-boiled eggs
1 cup light olive oil
2 tablespoons vinegar (white)

Mix asparagus tips with crawfish tails or shrimp and season with salt and pepper. Rub through a sieve the yolks of the hard-boiled eggs. Add enough oil and vinegar to make it the consistency of cream (beat very well). Pour over the salad and serve.

Modern Cooking Tip: If using food processor to make dressing, slowly drizzle oil through the feed tube.

Celery Salad

Makes 4 servings.
3 cups finely cut celery
1 cup cubed tart apple
½ cup cooked chestnuts, sliced
⅓–½ cup mayonnaise or french dressing

Mix finely cut celery and sour apple with (peeled) boiled chestnut slices. Serve with (⅓ to ½ cup) french dressing or mayonnaise.

Modern Cooking Tip: Canned chestnuts may be substituted.

Chiffonade Salad

Makes 4 servings.
1 cup shredded lettuce
1 cup chopped celery
1 cup shredded chicory (or escarole)
1 tablespoon each: chopped beets, onion, fresh parsley, dried tarragon, and sweet red pepper
4 crisp lettuce leaves
⅓–½ cup french dressing
Sliced tomato to garnish

Mix lettuce, celery, and chicory (or escarole) and chopped beets, onion, parsley, tarragon, and sweet red pepper. Serve on crisp lettuce, with french dressing, garnishing with sliced tomato.

Watercress Salad

Makes 4 servings.
1 pint (2 cups) watercress (4 bunches)
3 tablespoons oil (salad)
1 tablespoon vinegar (white wine)

¼ teaspoon salt
⅛ teaspoon pepper

Wash cress, snap off all decayed leaves, break in lengths about 2 inches, shake dry, and arrange on cold dish. Dress with oil, vinegar, and a dust of salt and pepper. Dandelion greens, oyster plant, chicory, escarole, and nasturtium leaves can be used in the same way.

Jardinière Salad

Mrs. Glessner once sent a novel gift (perhaps a peace offering) to a friend: a wreath devised from beets, lettuce, and peas in the pod, delivered with the note, "I am beeten . . . lettuce have peas."

Makes 4 servings.
3 cups cooked diced vegetables
Minced fine herbs (¼ teaspoon each: tarragon, basil, parsley—either fresh or dried)
4 crisp lettuce or watercress leaves
⅓ cup mayonnaise or french dressing (see recipe, p. 123)

Use diced cooked carrots, okra, beets, and cauliflower, turnips, peas, potatoes, beans, and asparagus tips, any or all. Sprinkle with minced fine herbs and serve on lettuce or cress with french dressing or mayonnaise.

Tomato Jelly Salad
Shortall Family Recipe

Makes 4–6 servings.
2 tablespoons (2 packets) unflavored gelatin
½ cup cold water
2 teaspoons salt
3 peppercorns
½ cup cut-up onion
3 cloves
1 bay leaf
1 28-ounce can tomatoes with juice or 3 cups tomato juice

Rind of 1 lemon (1 tablespoon)
4–6 crisp lettuce leaves
¼ cup mayonnaise

Soak gelatin in cold water till soft (5 minutes). Cook tomatoes and seasonings, except salt, 20 minutes. Strain and add salt. Pour hot over softened gelatin. Stir till dissolved. Pour into molds that have been wet with cold water. (Refrigerate 2–3 hours to gel.) Serve cold (unmolded) on lettuce leaves with mayonnaise.

Modern Cooking Tip: Tomatoes may be pureed in a blender for smoother consistency.

French Dressing

Makes 2 pints.
½ can tomato soup
¼ cup sugar
¾ teaspoon salt
⅛ teaspoon paprika
¼ teaspoon dry mustard
1 teaspoon onion juice
1 teaspoon Worcestershire sauce
¼ cup vinegar (white)
¾ cup olive oil

Mix all ingredients well.

Modern Cooking Tip: Mix in blender at high speed for best results. Chopped onion may be substituted for onion juice.

Tarragon Salad Dressing
Shortall Family Recipe

Although the proportions called for in this recipe yield a very small amount of dressing, it is easily doubled.

Makes about ⅓ cup.

4 tablespoons oil (salad)
1 tablespoon cider vinegar
¼ teaspoon dry mustard
¼ teaspoon sugar
Salt and pepper to taste
⅛ teaspoon crushed dried tarragon
¼ teaspoon chopped chives

Mix thoroughly. You may like more or less vinegar.

Modern Cooking Tip: In testing variation of this recipe, we preferred tarragon vinegar to the cider vinegar called for originally.

Mayonnaise Dressing

Makes about ¾ cup.

Yolks of 2 eggs
½ teaspoon salt
1 teaspoon dry mustard
Pinch of cayenne pepper
¼ pint (½ cup) best olive oil
1 tablespoon vinegar (white)
Juice ¼ lemon (1 tablespoon)

Put eggs in a china (nonmetal) bowl, salt and mustard, then (add cayenne), stir with a fork, and drop in the oil slowly till it thickens. Then add the vinegar and lemon juice, stirring all the time until well mixed. The juice of lemon may be substituted for vinegar.

Modern Cooking Tip: For best results, beat the ingredients with a hand mixer or in a blender. A whole egg may be substituted for the two yolks required.

Reverend Sydney Smith's love of good food prompted him to learn to cook. He soon became convinced that vice could be thwarted and virtue enhanced by proper eating. Character traits, said the good British Reverend, "are powerfully affected by beef, mutton, pie-crust, and rich soups." Although he never gave up preaching the virtues of a sensible diet from the pulpit and on parish rounds, his culinary triumph was salad making, prompting him to turn his popular recipe for salad dressing into a poem for Eliza Acton's 1830s cookbook, Modern Cookery:

To make this condiment your
   poet begs
The pounded yellow of two
   hard-boiled eggs;
Two boiled potatoes, strained
   through kitchen sieve,
Smoothness and softness to
   the salad give.

❧ Creamy Salad Dressing

Makes about 2½ cups.
1½ cups vinegar (white)
Butter the size of an egg (¼ cup)
1 teaspoon salt
⅛ teaspoon cayenne pepper
6 eggs, beaten lightly
1 cup cream
1 tablespoon of sugar

Put vinegar and butter in a saucepan and set it in boiling water. Add the salt and pepper, mustard if desired. When nearly boiling, stir in very slowly the eggs beaten lightly. Great care must be taken that it does not curdle. When ready to serve, add cream and sugar.

❧ Cooked Salad Dressing

Makes about ¾ cup.
1 tablespoon mustard (prepared)
2 eggs
½ teaspoon salt
Pinch of pepper
1 teaspoon sugar
½ teacup (¼ cup) melted butter
½ coffee cup (½ cup) vinegar (white)

Rub the mustard thoroughly into the eggs (mixing well), add salt, pepper, and sugar, then the melted butter, a few drops at a time; lastly, the vinegar very slowly. Cook until smooth and thickened. (Heat over a low flame for about 5 minutes. Serve warm with spinach salad.)

Let onion atoms lurk within
    the bowl,
And half-suspected, animate
    the whole.
Of mordant mustard add a
    single spoon,
Distrust the condiment that
    bites so soon;
But deem it not, thou man of
    herbs, a fault
To add a double quality of
    salt;
Four times the spoon with oil
    of Lucca crown,
And twice with vinegar
    procur'd from town;
And lastly o'er the flavor'd
    compound toss
A magic soupçon of anchovy
    sauce.
Oh, green and glorious! Oh,
    herbaceous treat!
Twould tempt the dying
    anchorite to eat;
Back to the world he'd turn
    his fleeting soul,
And plunge his fingers in the
    salad-bowl!
Serenely full, the epicure
    would say,
"Fate cannot harm me, I have
    dined today.

23. Glessner House dry pantry, showing the door to the cold room *on the left*.

Sauces, Pickles, and Preserves

White Sauce

Glessner Family Recipe

Makes 1¾–2 cups.

6 ounces (¾ cup) butter (½ cup reserved)
1 ounce (2 tablespoons) flour
Salt, pepper, and nutmeg to taste
1 pint (2 cups) boiling water
Juice of 1 lemon (¼ cup)

Work together ¼ cup butter and the flour in a saucepan (over a low flame, not allowing it to brown). Add salt, pepper, and a trifle of nutmeg; pour in boiling water, stir, and boil a minute. Strain and add (reserved) butter and the lemon juice.

Modern Cooking Tip: This sauce is actually more a butter sauce or sauce bâtard than a white sauce. Water can be replaced with an equal amount of milk, chicken stock, or veal stock (see recipe, p. 48) for a richer sauce.

One night, hurrying to be punctual, the Robert Pecks and two other guests were stopped by a traffic officer and given the rough side of his tongue for speeding. "But officer," exclaimed Mrs. Peck, "we are going to Mrs. Glessner's for dinner and we're late." "Ah, if that's the way of it, you should have told me that in the first place," the policeman responded and sped the party on its way.

Mrs. Frances Glessner found it helpful to keep detailed lists of dinner guests and the menus she served them, which she maintained in bound journals from 1892 until her death in 1932. In this manner she could avoid the social blunder of repeatedly serving the same menu items to her frequent guests.

Allemande Sauce for Beef

Glessner Family Recipe

Makes about 2½ cups.
1 pint (2 cups) white sauce (see recipe, p. 127)
1 tablespoon mushroom catsup (see recipe, p. 133)
Salt and pepper to taste
Trifle of nutmeg (pinch of nutmeg, to taste)
1 tablespoon butter
6 egg yolks
½ cup cream
Juice of half a lemon (2 tablespoons)

Let the sauce heat in another pan of boiling water (double boiler) and add all the seasoning except the lemon (mushroom catsup, salt, pepper, nutmeg, and butter). Beat the yolks of the eggs and the cream together and add to the sauce. Stir 3 minutes, take off, and add the lemon juice. Strain and pour over the fillet.

Modern Cooking Tip: Putting the mixture through a blender when done will improve smoothness. Canned mushroom soup stock can be substituted for mushroom catsup.

Currant Jelly Sauce for Lamb

Shortall Family Recipe

Makes about 1 cup, serving four.
4 tablespoons butter, melted
½ cup currant jelly
½ teaspoon mustard (prepared) or 1 teaspoon lemon juice
Salt and cayenne pepper to taste

Mix all ingredients well together. Cut cold mutton in very thin slices and heat in this sauce.

❧ Raisin Sauce for Ham

Shortall Family Recipe

Makes 2–2½ cups.
¾ **cup raisins**
4–5 cloves
1 cup water
1 teaspoon cornstarch
¾ **cup sugar**
Dash of pepper
1 tablespoon lemon juice
1 tablespoon vinegar (white)
1 tablespoon butter

Heat raisins and cloves in water. Add cornstarch mixed with a little cold water (about 1 tablespoon), sugar, pepper. When slightly thickened, add lemon juice and vinegar, and, last of all, the butter. (Heat, stirring constantly, for about 5 minutes.)

❧ Fruit Sauce for Ham

Makes about 1 cup.
¾ **cup crushed pineapple**
¼ **cup seedless raisins**
¼ **cup orange juice**
1 tablespoon grated orange rind
¼ **cup brown sugar**

(Mix all ingredients well.) Simmer gently 10 minutes and pour hot sauce over sliced ham when serving.

❧ Pickled Watermelon

Harvey Family Recipe

1 watermelon
1 teaspoon alum per gallon of melon
1 tablespoon salt per gallon of melon

Amid the hectic social life of the late 1800s and early 1900s in Chicago, an eligible bachelor for many hostesses was one who could be counted on to come to dinner. Bachelors dined out every night of their lives, and most of them did not live man's allotted time. "Late hours and a confusion of sauces," mused Arthur Meeker, Jr., "must have accounted for their comparatively early departure from the scene."

1 pint (2 cups) vinegar (white)
1 quart sugar
11 teaspoons mixed (pickling) spices (2 teaspoons
reserved)

Peel (melon) and cut up the rind. Cover with water.
Then boil with powdered alum and salt. Strain. To
pickle, boil up once vinegar, sugar, and (9 teaspoons or
3 tablespoons) spices in muslin bag (cheesecloth). Then
put melon in the syrup, throw in (reserved 2
teaspoons) spices, and let boil once. Put in jars and
seal while hot (seal in canning jar according to
manufacturer's direction).

Pickled Beets

2 cups vinegar (white)
1 blade mace (about ½ teaspoon)
1 teaspoon ground ginger or about ½-inch fresh
ginger
1 teaspoon prepared horseradish
4 cups sliced cooked beets

Having cooked the beets . . . cut them into pieces of
even size. Boil vinegar enough to cover them in a jar,
with mace, ginger, and horseradish; pour it boiling hot
to the sliced beets and cork down when cold (seal in
canning jar according to manufacturer's directions;
refrigerate).

Modern Cooking Tip: To cook beets boil about 10
whole, unpeeled beets in water to cover. Simmer for
40–45 minutes, until fork tender. Drain, keep under
running water until cool enough to handle, remove
skin, and slice. This will yield the 4 cups of sliced
beets required above.

❧Pickled Sweet Corn Ears

This is a recipe for what today would be called "pickled baby corn." We include it for historical reference—and for those few lucky enough to have fresh baby corn available to them. Ingredients are basic, and proportions should be adjusted according to the supply of baby corn to be preserved.

Baby corn ears
White vinegar to cover
Pinch of salt

Take the "nubbins" of early corn where there are too many forming on the stalk, while very small and tender. Trim neatly and boil them 5 minutes in water slightly salted. Drain and put them in a jar. Boil good white vinegar enough to cover and pour it boiling hot over the corn. Let it remain so until the next day. Then boil vinegar again, adding a little salt; fill up the jar with it when partially cold. Cork the jar and seal it (seal in canning jar according to manufacturer's directions).

❧ Pickled Carrots

2 pounds baby carrots
2 cups vinegar (white)
1 bayleaf
3–4 cloves
Pinch of salt

Take small carrots (slender variety), such as first come to market in bunches in summer. Scald them and rub and wash off the skin. Parboil them in salted water (to cover, until fork will just pierce the skin), drain, and put them in a jar. Boil vinegar enough to cover them, pour it in, and let remain so 24 hours. Then drain off the vinegar and boil again. Put bay leaf and cloves in

Florence Pullman Miller, granddaughter of George M. Pullman, learned from her grandmother's diary that on a summer's day in New Jersey, Mrs. Pullman had put on an apron and "made peaches into sweet pickles and put up grape preserves." It was difficult for Mrs. Miller to picture her grandmother in such a role because in memory she was "always so dressed up it was hard to believe she ever set foot in the kitchen."

with the carrots, add a little salt to the boiling vinegar, and pour it to the carrots again. Cork down the jar when nearly cold and seal it (seal in canning jar according to manufacturer's directions; refrigerate). These pickled young carrots are as good as pickled beets, care being taken not to get them cooked soft when parboiling them, and they add another color and ornament to the salad dishes and supper table.

Grated Cucumber Pickle

1 dozen large cucumbers
3 teaspoons salt (2 teaspoons reserved)
3 onions
3 green peppers
4 cups vinegar (white)

Pare (cucumbers), cut open, scrape out all the seeds. Then grate (or thinly slice). Make a bag of cheesecloth like a jelly bag, hang the pulp up overnight to drain. Chop fine the onions and green peppers. Use salt according to taste (about 2 teaspoons) and add to the pulp a quart of best vinegar. (Seal in canning jar according to manufacturer's directions).

Modern Cooking Tip: In lieu of hanging the pulp up to drain overnight, mix with 1 teaspoon of salt and set in colander to drain for 2–3 hours, then rinse.

Cold Tomato Relish

Harvey Family Recipe

The Harvey's coachman, John, went with the family to Mackinac Island for the summers, leaving behind his wife and daughter to put up preserves and jellies for the family storeroom.

1 peck (5 quarts) ripe tomatoes, peeled, chopped fine, and drained
2 cups chopped onions
2 cups chopped celery
2 cups sugar
1 cup mustard seed

½ cup salt
1 teaspoon powdered mace
1 teaspoon pepper
4 teaspoons ground cinnamon
4 red (bell) peppers, chopped fine
2 quarts (8 cups) vinegar (white)

Put in stone jar and cover tightly (seal in canning jar according to manufacturer's directions). Ready for use in 6 weeks.

Modern Cooking Tip: To prepare for sealing, just mix all ingredients together, by hand or using a 2-pronged cooking fork, in a large nonaluminum bowl.

Mushroom Catsup

Makes ½ cup.
3 pounds mushrooms, cleaned
2½ tablespoons salt
½ teaspoon whole pepper
6 cloves
2 teaspoons ginger
⅓ cup white vinegar

Break up (dice) the required quantity of mushrooms, put them in a tub, salt over, and leave for 2 days. Afterward, take out all the juice (by straining pulp) into a saucepan. Put in peppercorns, cloves, and ginger (in a cheesecloth tied with a string. Add vinegar.) When boiling, move the catsup to the side of the fire and let it simmer gently (for ½ hour).

Modern Cooking Tip: A much simpler method of making this sauce is to use a blender. Place the mushrooms in a blender with 1 cup of water and blend to a thick brown pulp. Strain pulp for juice and add salt. Then add spices in cheesecloth, and vinegar, and bring to boil. Allow to cool, discard the pulp, package and freeze any extra. This recipe yields a liquid, not a stock, consistency.

The term ketchup, *also* catsup, *is derived from the Chinese* ket-tsiap, *meaning "pickled fish sauce," which was picked up by English sailors in the seventeenth century and first mentioned in print in 1711.*

 *Oyster Catsup*

2 dozen whole shucked oysters
3 anchovies (filleted)
½ teaspoon each: ground cloves, cayenne pepper,
and ground mace
2 cups white wine
2 wineglasses (1 cup) brandy

Pound oysters with anchovies in a mortar and season
with cloves, cayenne pepper, and mace. Mix their
(oysters) liquor with them, turn them into a lined
(nonaluminum) saucepan, pour in wine and brandy.
Place the catsup over a slow fire until boiling, then
strain it through a fine sieve. When cold, pour the
catsup into bottles and keep them tightly corked for
use.

Modern Cooking Tip: Oysters may be cleaned and
pureed in a food processor or blender.

Whole Preserved Apples

At the summer home of the Glessners in New Hampshire, the servants (city girls from Chicago) picked the blackberries, raspberries, gooseberries, currants, and other fruits as they ripened, and made jams, jellies, and other preserves, all brought back to Prairie Avenue in the private railway car in which the family and staff traveled.

2¼–2½ pounds large firm apples
4 cups water
3 cups sugar
1 teaspoon lemon peel or orange peel
½ teaspoon mace

Peel and core large firm apples; pippins are best.
Throw them into water as you pare them. Boil the
parings in water for 15 minutes. Then strain (remove
apples from soaking water and put into a strainer).
Add (to cooking water) sugar, with enough lemon or
orange peel and mace to impart a pleasant flavor;
return to the kettle. (Bring to a boil, reduce to
simmer, and cook about 20 minutes until syrupy,
skimming as white foam forms.) When the syrup has
been well skimmed and is clear, put it boiling hot over
the apples, which must be drained from the water in

which they have hitherto stood (dried and put into jars). Then let them remain in the syrup until both are perfectly cold (seal and refrigerate). When all the minutiae of these directions are attended to, the fruit will remain unbroken and present a beautiful and inviting appearance.

Modern Cooking Tip: Modern canning techniques should be followed if apples are to be keep unrefrigerated.

Spiced Peaches (Or Any Small Fruit)
Meeker Family Recipe

5 pounds fruit
4 cups water
8 cups sugar
3 tablespoons vinegar (white)
4 tablespoons ground cinnamon
1 heaping teaspoon ground cloves

If using peaches, they must be peeled, stoned, and quartered first. Then add sugar. Put (fruit) into porcelain (nonaluminum) kettle and cook slowly (in water) until fruit is well cooked (fork tender). Then skim out the fruit (remove from kettle) and let syrup cook down until it is quite thick; then add vinegar, ground cinnamon, and ground cloves. Mix the spices thoroughly with the syrup and add the peaches. Let it get hot (2–3 minutes) and can it up (seal in canning jar according to manufacturer's directions).

Rhubarb Marmalade

Anderson Family Recipe

4 pounds rhubarb, chucked
½ pound shelled walnuts
6 oranges, chopped with peel
12 cups sugar

Boil all first without sugar until rhubarb and oranges are cooked. Then add sugar and boil until thick.

Mincemeat

Anderson Family Recipe

Mincemeat is a favorite holiday tradition recalled by the descendants of Prairie Avenue families. On one occasion, when the men at the Armour plant had to work through Christmas day, Philip Armour had mince pies dispatched for them from his home. But perhaps the best word on mincemeat was written by Mrs. Glessner in her 1886 Christmas morning alphabet:

M is for mince meat
Which many a prince eats
With brandy and plums
And extra dry Mumms!

This traditional Prairie Avenue favorite makes an easy and elegant Christmas gift.

Makes about 6 quarts.
2 pounds (5⅓ cups) raisins, stoned (seeded)
2 pounds (5⅓ cups) currants, well washed
4 pounds apples (peeled, cored, and chopped)
2 pounds suet, chopped fine
1 pound lean beef, chopped
1 pound almonds, chopped
1 pound mixed citron and lemon (candied peel)
2 oranges (1 cup orange juice; 2 tablespoons grated orange rind)
3 lemons (¾ cup lemon juice; 1 tablespoon grated lemon rind)
1 (4 cups) quart cider
1 pint (2 cups) brandy
1 large (heaping) tablespoon (each) of mixed spices: cinnamon, mace, and cloves
1 tablespoon salt
4 pounds (8 cups) sugar

(Mix all ingredients together well.) Cook slowly for 2 hours, stirring often (bring to a boil, then simmer for

2–3 hours, or until thickened). Store in sealed jars
(seal in canning jar with removable lid according to
manufacturer's directions.)

Modern Cooking Tip: For a more pungent
mincemeat, add brandy after cooking and reheat
almost to a boiling point in a pressure cooker.
Exercise caution when heating flammable liquids like
brandy. With this method, mincemeat should age for a
minimum of 2 weeks, preferably a month.

24. George Pullman twins, George, Jr., and Sanger, in matching button suits.

Prairie
Avenue
Children

In contrast to the formal social extravaganzas of Prairie Avenue's adult residents are the simpler joys of its children: marking the walks for games of hopscotch with used carbons discarded by the lamplighter, hitching rides on the ice wagon, and searching for remnants of the Fort Dearborn Massacre, which had taken place on the site in 1812. When a monument commemorating that battle was set up at the edge of the Pullman estate, "it became a favorite gathering place for nursemaids and kids jumping rope," Katherine Shortall Dunbaugh recalled years later. "We held very heated discussions about that statue . . . which Indians were the 'good guys' and which 'the bad.'"

Some Prairie Avenue children were privately schooled at home by tutors, such as the Glessners' two children, George and Frances. Mr. Glessner recalled, "The schoolroom . . . was a rendezvous for . . . friends and teachers alike, for they were all comrades together. . . . Over the thresholds passed a regular procession of teachers . . . in literature, languages, humanities, and the practical, considerably beyond the curricula of the High Schools." His pride was apparently justified, when his son went on to attend college at Harvard.

Other privileged children on the street enjoyed well-appointed nurseries and playrooms. Burton Holmes remembered in awe an afternoon that he and his sister passed playing in the nursery of Ethel Field, the daughter of Marshall Field, who would one day become a leader of London society as the wife of Admiral Lord Beatty. "I recall," he wrote in his autobiography, "being overwhelmed by the variety and costliness of the toys in the Field nursery and playroom."

Neighborhood pets included pigeons, ponies, and an occasional tethered cow or cooped pig. The Meeker and Harvey children had

25. Glessner House schoolroom.

baby alligators sent from Florida, which the girls pushed in their doll buggies, hoping to startle overly curious adults. Young Phil Sears kept a lamb and a goat in his family's mansion and reportedly once brought the Pullman's dog home for a bath in one of the family's tubs.

Upon visiting the Field Museum each Sunday afternoon, young Daphne Field regularly disappeared upon reaching the taxidermy department and had to be searched for through the length and breadth of the museum. "I never could understand," said her sister Katherine, "why no one realized it was that awful smell that sent her flying." The girls traveled about town in a carriage pulled by a high-stepping piebald named Tickle and often played strenuous games of hide-and-seek on the grounds of the Potter Palmer mansion. In winter they sported chic gray squirrel coats, but no leggings. "My mother was from Baltimore," explained Katherine Field Rodman. "From the beginning, she considered Chicago's climate vile, and couldn't see how her children were to survive unless they were 'hardened.'"

Two blocks to the north lived Bishop Anderson of the Episcopal diocese, for whose children life was even stricter. No roller skating and no bike riding on Sunday, and no theatre during Lent (which meant missing Maude Adams in *Peter Pan*). Most trying of all during adolescence, the bishop's daughters were expected to stop dancing at the stroke of midnight, whatever the occasion. Decades later, Katherine Anderson Sulzberger still remembered the "Cinderella" taunts that resulted.

There were unwritten rules for other Prairie Avenue children as well, as ten-year-old Katherine Shortall learned when she went downtown alone for her piano lesson. Passing the windows of the Chicago Club, young Katherine waved happily at her grandfather, who seemed to look through her and then turned his back. That evening, as she and her brothers and sisters were nibbling bread and jelly at their little table in the family dining room, Grandfather Shortall dropped in for a visit. "My dear Katherine," he exclaimed, "when a lady passes the window of a gentleman's club, she never looks up. For when a gentleman is in his club, he is invisible."

Children were seldom allowed at Prairie Avenue dinner tables when guests were present, but they usually managed to sneak a glimpse of the comings and goings. Remembrances are filled with accounts of peeking from behind curtains, through doors, and over

26. *Left to right:* Ethel Field, Alice Keith, and Florence Otis dressed for the Mikado Ball given by the Marshall Field family for the children of Prairie Avenue, ca. 1886. Ethel Field lived at 1905 Prairie Avenue, Alice Keith at 1901 Prairie Avenue, and Florence Otis at 1730 Prairie Avenue.

balustrades to catch sight of the endless parade of dignitaries: divas and poets, architects and archbishops, intellectuals and nobility.

Prairie Avenue children were introduced to the social graces at Professor A. E. Bournique's dance academy. A dapper man usually turned out in full dress, Monsieur Bournique always clutched a clapper that he used to beat the rhythm of each dance. Children as young as six were taught the Highland fling, the sailor's hornpipe, and the Cupid's trumpet. They came for individual lessons and group lessons and, in time, advanced to the two-step, the waltz, and the intricacies of the cotillion. Young ladies were advised not to accept invitations for every dance: "The fatigue is too wearing, and the heated faces that it induces too unbecoming," cautioned *Sensible Etiquette of the Best Society*. Young Burton Holmes discovered that some of his peers took this advice seriously during one dance class. He later recalled little Hattie Pullman, the youngest daughter of George Pullman, refusing to dance with him as "the first social snub of my life."

27. Mrs. Glessner's Monday Morning Reading Class in the courtyard of Glessner House, ca. 1902. Mrs. Glessner stands *on upper porch*, fourth figure *from the left*, next to the class's reader, Miss Sybil Trimmingham, fifth figure *from the left*.

Cakes

❧ Coconut Cakes

1 cup (½ pound) butter
3 cups sugar (confectioners')
3 cups flour, sifted
3 teaspoons baking powder (sifted with 1
teaspoon salt into flour)
½ cup sweet (whole) milk
Whites of 10 eggs, well beaten (until stiff soft
peaks)

Beat butter and sugar to a cream (with an electric beater, or by hand, until light and fluffy). Add flour, baking powder, and milk (add flour and baking powder mixture alternately with milk); last, stir in the eggs very lightly (fold only until blended). Do not be concerned if batter looks very raw and dry before folding in eggs. Bake in a moderate oven in two 1-inch-deep greased and floured 8-inch round cake pans (350 degrees for 25–35 minutes, or until toothpick comes out clean). Makes 2 cakes.

Modern Cooking Tip: For an interesting flavor twist and to approximate the "sweet" milk of the day, which had a higher cream content than our milk today, try coconut milk. (If using canned coconut cream, the addition of salt to baking powder is not necessary.)

For more than thirty years, Chicago women gathered weekly in Glessner House for Mrs. Glessner's famed Monday Morning Reading Class. Luncheon was served to the class one Monday each month. A member of the class later recalled that Mrs. Glessner's meals were so memorable no one ever missed the class on luncheon days. One of many treats relished by members of the class was a coconut cake "so good it was sinful."

ICING

Whites of 3 eggs
1 pound sugar (2 cups), sifted
Juice of 1 small lemon (3 tablespoons)
¾ cup grated coconut

Beat the eggs to a stiff froth, then add the sugar and lemon juice. Put 1 layer cake on a stand. While warm, spread on the icing, then sprinkle thick with coconut. Lay the other cake on top and do the same. (Repeat icing process.) At the last, spread icing all over the top and edges and put on as much coconut as will adhere.

Modern Cooking Tip: Modern nutritionists caution against the use of raw egg whites because of the danger of salmonella. As a safer substitute for turn-of-the-century icings that use uncooked egg whites, we offer the following cooked variation to which recipe-specific ingredients such as grated coconut and lemon juice can then be added:

1 cup whipping cream
1 cup sugar
Yolks of 3 eggs, beaten
½ cup butter
1 tablespoon vanilla

Combine cream, sugar, yolks, butter, and vanilla. Over medium heat, cook and stir 10–12 minutes, until thick. Add 1 cup grated coconut flakes and juice of 1 lemon. Cool by plunging into large bowl of ice cubes, stirring constantly until thick enough to spread or add 1 cup of confectioners' sugar to thicken. Spread on cake and sprinkle with coconut flakes.

❧ Black Christmas Cake

Anderson Family Recipe

Makes 1 cake.

1 pound (2⅔ cups) raisins, when stoned (seeded)
1 pound (2⅔ cups) currants
¼ cup brandy
½ pound (1 cup) sugar
⅔ pound (1¼ cup) butter
5 eggs
⅔ pound (a scant 2¼ cups) flour
½ dessert spoon (¼ tablespoon) baking soda
¼ cup wine (red table wine)

Mix all ingredients together and bake in a slow oven (275 degrees in an 8½-by-4½-by-2½-inch loaf pan) 3½ hours.

Modern Cooking Tip: To prepare for baking: Soak raisins and currants in brandy, set aside. Cream butter and sugar with an electric beater or by hand. Add eggs. Sift flour and baking soda in and fold to blend. Add wine and fold in raisin mixture. (Bake in well-greased bundt pan). After baking, brush cake with a little brandy while warm and let cool in pan. This yields a densely textured cake more like a fruit cake.

On February 9, 1898, nineteen-year-old Frances Glessner married Blewett Lee in an afternoon ceremony held in the parlor of her parent's Prairie Avenue home. At the reception that followed, guests were served pyramids of black and white cake, frozen eggnog, claret, tea, coffee, small cakes shaped like hearts, bonbons with white bow knots on top, and sandwiches. On top of the cake pyramids were small bride and groom figurines that had adorned her parents' wedding cake in 1870.

❧ Angel Food Cake

Harvey Family Recipe

Makes 1 cake.

Whites of 11 large eggs
1½ tumblers (cups) granulated sugar, sifted 4 or 5 times
1 teaspoon cream of tartar, added to sugar toward the last of the sifting
1 teaspoon vanilla
1 tumbler (cup) flour, sifted 3 times

It is reputed that angel food cake was introduced to Chicago, fittingly enough, by the mother of a South Side clergyman.

Beat egg whites (thoroughly until stiff, but not dry, glossy peaks begin to form). Sift in sugar gradually, beating eggs all the time. Add vanilla after sugar. Then put in flour the same way (sift in gradually while beating.) Bake about an hour in an oven right for bread (in an ungreased 10-inch tube pan). Put thick brown paper on top. Do not call to have it brown until about 10 minutes before it is done. Then remove paper.

Modern Cooking Tip: The use of the paper bag to control browning is not necessary in the modern oven. Best results are achieved when the cake is baked at 350 degrees for approximately 45 minutes.

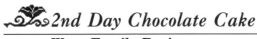

2nd Day Chocolate Cake

Ware Family Recipe

The name of this cake serves as notice to users that it truly is tastier on the day after making.

Makes 2 cakes, layered.

½ **cup cocoa**
1½ **cups sugar**
1 **cup milk**
½ **cup shortening (vegetable)**
2 **eggs, separated**
2 **cups flour**
1 **teaspoon baking soda (sifted with ½ teaspoon salt into flour)**
1 **teaspoon cream of tartar (optional, sifted into flour)**
1 **teaspoon vanilla**

(Bake each layer cake in 375-degree oven for 30–35 minutes in greased 9-inch round pans.)

Modern Cooking Tip: For a richer cake, substitute buttermilk for whole milk. To prepare ingredients for baking: Blend ½ cup sugar, ½ cup cocoa, and ½ cup milk well and set aside. Cream shortening and remaining cup of sugar together with an electric beater or by hand. Beat in egg yolks, cocoa mixture, and flour. Add remaining ½ cup milk and vanilla. Lightly fold in egg whites beaten stiff, not dry. Check cake after it has baked for 25 minutes. Cake is done when it begins to pull away from the sides of the pan, or when tester comes out clean. Put one cake on stand and spread icing on top while warm. Lay on second layer cake and repeat icing process. Then spread icing all over top and edges.

ICING
4 ounces unsweetened chocolate
1 cup confectioners' sugar, sifted
2 eggs
1 teaspoon vanilla extract or brandy

Melt chocolate, add confectioners' sugar. Beat in eggs, one at a time (with wire whisk over a low flame until smooth). Stir in vanilla extract or brandy.

English Walnut Cake
Columbian Exposition Cookbook

All that remained of this turn-of-the-century recipe were the concepts and the ingredients, around which the recipe has been reconstructed.

Makes 1 cake.
½ cup butter
2 cups sugar
4 eggs
3 cups flour
2 teaspoons baking powder
1½ cups milk

While traveling through Europe with her mother in 1894, Bessie Keith described the following incident in Belgium: "We went . . . to Antwerp to see the fair, which although is [a] mere toy as compared with the World's Fair [World's Columbian Exposition], nevertheless surprised us a great deal—we saw some of the Turks from the Midway Plaisance and the minute we said "Bum Bum" their faces brightened up and I think we might have had most anything just for the asking."

Cream butter, with an electric mixer or by hand. Mix in sugar well. Add eggs one at a time, beating well after each addition. Add remaining dry ingredients and milk alternately, ending with milk. Mix only until blended. Pour into greased and floured 9-by-13-by-2-inch pan. Bake at 350 degrees for 50–60 minutes, or until cake tests done. Let cool on wire rack for 10 minutes, then remove from pan and allow to cool completely.

ICING

1 cup semisweet chocolate (6 ounces chocolate chips)
2 tablespoons butter
1 cup powdered sugar
3 tablespoons hot milk or cream
1 tablespoon vanilla
½ pound (1 cup) walnut meats

In heavy pan over low heat, combine chocolate and butter until smooth and melted. Remove from heat. Add sugar and beat well until smooth. Add hot milk and vanilla; beat until smooth and cooler. Spread over cake and place walnuts over.

Seed Cake

Shortall Family Recipe

Makes 1 cake.

2 cups flour
2 cups sugar
1 cup butter
2 eggs
2 teaspoons baking powder
¾ ounce (about 3 teaspoons) caraway seeds
Nutmeg to taste (about ½ to 1 teaspoon)
Milk enough to make into a batter (¼ cup)

Cream together sugar and butter, add beaten eggs. Then mix all dry ingredients together well, add to cream mixture, and pour into loaf pan and bake for approximately an hour at 325 degrees.

Fruit Cake Blitz

Glessner Family Recipe

Makes 1 9-inch cake.
⅓ cup shortening
3 tablespoon sugar
1 egg
1 cup sifted flour
1 teaspoon baking powder
Pinch of salt
½ teaspoon vanilla
Any choice of fresh fruit—chopped (or sliced)

Cream shortening and sugar. Add egg and beat well. Sift flour with baking powder, add salt (and add to the creamed shortening). Add vanilla and mix. Spread in a (9-inch-square baking) pan with floured fingers. Cover with any fruit. Bake at 350–375 degrees for about 25 minutes.

Individual Cheesecakes

Makes 8 servings.
½ pound cheese (cream)
1 cup butter
2 cups flour
½ cup sugar
Chopped nuts (to garnish)

Cream the cheese and butter thoroughly. Add sugar and flour gradually and let the mixture stand in the icebox until the next morning. Roll out the mixture

On one memorable morning, members of Mrs. Glessner's Monday Morning Reading Class paid a charming tribute to their hostess. They arrived in procession, each carrying a single rose to lay in the arms of their hostess, who was poised to greet them at the door, until she stood with her arms filled with roses.

(between 2 sheets of wax paper) about ⅓ of an inch thick. Cut it into strips 1 inch wide and 3 inches long, sprinkle with nuts, and refrigerate until serving.

Modern Cooking Tip: Cream cheese may be creamed by hand or with the aid of a food processor, blender, or electric mixer.

Turn-of-the-Century Cheesecake

Procure a calf's rennet, such as the cheesemakers use, from the butcher, put a piece the size of two fingers into a vial, fill up with water. When it has stood a few hours, strain the rennet water into a pan of new milk and stir to mix. In two or three hours, the milk will turn to curds and whey. Set the pan over a slow fire to get hot without scorching at bottom, and without stirring. When at the boiling point, pour the curd into a napkin set in a strainer, tie, and hang up to drip dry. This curd is good for a number of excellent articles.

For cheesecakes, take: 12 ounces of curd, 4 ounces of sugar, 3 ounces of butter, 4 yolks of eggs, lemon rind grated, grated nutmeg, and a pinch of salt. Rub the curd, as taken from the draining cloth, through a flour sieve, mash it together. Line patty pans with paste, nearly fill with the mixture, bake about 15 minutes. The curd mixture, though seemingly too firm at first, melts and puffs up in the oven. Dredge powdered sugar over the tops when done.

As substitutes for rennet curd, which is as sweet as pounded almonds, the curd of sour milk or the curd of a custard that is spoiled through letting it boil can be used if prepared by scalding and draining in the same way, but it will not be quite so good.

❧ Updated Cheesecake Recipe

For those without calf's rennet in the pantry, or who have trouble sorting their curds from their whey, we offer the following modern rendition of this recipe. It produces a small, flat cake that is a good base for seasonal fruits. If to be eaten without fruit or other topping, the recipe benefits from doubling the amount of lemon rind.

Makes 1 cake.

18 ounces cream cheese, softened
¾ cup sugar
4½ tablespoons melted butter
6 egg yolks
¼ teaspoon grated lemon rind
Large pinch of grated nutmeg
Pinch of salt
Powdered sugar to top

Cream the cheese and sugar. Add butter and egg yolks and mix until blended. Add lemon rind, nutmeg, and salt. Mix thoroughly. Put into a well-greased 10-inch springform pan. Bake in a 350-degree oven for 35–45 minutes.

❧ Orange Cake

This recipe is a variation of the orange cake featured in the Columbian Exposition cookbook.

Makes 1 cake.

1 coffee cup (1 cup) sugar
½ coffee cup (½ cup) butter
4 eggs, separated
½ coffee cup (½ cup) milk
2 coffee cups (2 cups) flour
2 teaspoons baking powder

Cream sugar and butter together until light and fluffy (with an electric mixer or by hand). Add yolks of 4 eggs and blend. Add ⅓ of the milk. Add ½ of the flour and baking powder together. Add ⅓ of the milk. Add remaining flour and baking powder. Add remaining milk and mix only until blended. Beat whites of 2 eggs until peaks form, but not until dry. Fold gently into mixture and pour into well-greased and floured tube or bundt pan. Bake in a 350-degree oven for approximately 45 minutes, or until cake tests done.

ICING

Rind of 2 oranges (grated, no pith)
⅔ cup orange juice
1 coffee cup (1 cup) powdered sugar
Mix ingredients well and dribble over cake.

Sponge Cake

Harvey Family Recipe

Makes 1 cake.

3 eggs
1 cup sugar
1 cup flour, sifted
1 teaspoon baking powder (sifted into flour)
½ cup water

Separate eggs, beat sugar and whites together. Next add yolks, then flour and baking powder, adding the water last. Bake in an ungreased 9-inch baking pan at 325 degrees for minutes (for 30–40 minutes).

From a sponge cake recipe of the day: "Beat the sugar and eggs together with a stout wire egg whisk for half and hour ... The goodness of the cake depends altogether upon the beating. The best vessel is a bell-metal kettle, but a deep pan or pail will do."

ஃ*Huckleberry Cake*

Harvey Family Recipe

Makes 1 cake.

1 quart (4 cups) flour
1 cup sugar
3 teaspoons baking powder
½ teaspoon salt
Butter size of small egg (¼ cup)
1 quart berries
1½ cups milk

Work all together (flour, sugar, baking powder, salt, and butter) before putting in the berries. Then add milk. Have oven hot, and put in immediately. Bake about an hour (at 350 degrees in an 8½-by-4½-by-2½-inch loaf pan).

Modern Cooking Tip: Blueberries may be substituted for the rare huckleberry, a member of the same family. It also tastes very good with raspberries.

FROSTING

Glessner Family Recipe

1 egg
1 tablespoon cream
1 square melted chocolate
½ teaspoon vanilla
Powdered sugar (1¼–1½ cup)

Break an egg into a bowl and stir in enough powdered sugar to consistency suitable for spreading. Add cream, chocolate, and vanilla. Mix together until creamy. Apply to cake.

The dinner at which the Glessners discussed the commission for their new home on Prairie Avenue with famous architect Henry H. Richardson was crowned with the strawberry shortcake for which their cook was widely known. A more cultivated architect than epicure, Richardson asked for a second piece, adding, "Mrs. Glessner, that's the best pie I ever put in my mouth."

Strawberry Shortcake

1 cup sugar
1 tablespoon butter
1 heaping cup flour
¼ cup milk
3 eggs
1 teaspoon baking powder
1 quart fresh strawberries

Rub (cream) butter and sugar together, beat yolks separately, and add to mixture. Then add milk, flour, beaten egg whites, and baking powder. Bake in three jelly tins (loaf pans) at 450 degrees for 15–18 minutes and, when cold, place the berries between the layers, sprinkling them with sugar. Heap whipped cream upon the cake.

Pies and Tarts

❧ Wheatless Piecrust

Field Family Recipe

Makes 1 pie shell.

1 cup barley flour
½ cup butter
2–5 tablespoons cold water

For a single crust, take a cup barley flour. Rub enough butter into it to make it look like wet sand. Bind together with a little cold water. Roll out. Put on ice for half hour.

Modern Cooking Tip: Barley flour is available at health food stores. It is easier to use a pastry blender for mixing butter into the barley flour. This recipe yields a pastry with a less flaky and fuller texture than one made with regular white flour.

❧ Homemade Puff Pastry

Makes pastry for 2 pies.

¾ quart (3 cups) of flour
1½ coffee cups (¾ lb, or 1½ cups) of butter, hard
1 tablespoon sugar

This recipe came by way of the Shortall family, from Nora, cook at the Huron Mountain Club in Michigan. Pastry was often made in huge quantities—this one making enough for about 8 pies.

2½ pounds (5 cups) lard
1½ pounds (3 cups) butter
1 teaspoon salt
1 handful sugar
7 pounds (14 cups) flour
3 cups water

This dough does not require delicate handling at all in being rolled out. Mix all ingredients together with the hands in a large pan, then pack solidly in a flat enamel pan, covered with wax paper, and set in the bottom of the icebox, where it keeps for 6 weeks.

According to Nora, "There are three essentials to the making of good pastry. Cooks often leave out all

28. Glessner House kitchen.

Yolk of 1 egg
1 scant cup ice water
1 ice cube

Sift flour, add sugar; break the yolk of an egg into a pint bowl with a little ice water and a lump of ice, beat, and set to one side. Take the hard butter in cool fingertips, slice all in pieces about the size of a thumb into the flour. Then lightly and quickly take each floury lump of butter between thumb and finger and give it 1 rub, just enough to flatten, not more, leaving each piece separate. The egg and ice water should half fill the pint bowl (if necessary, add more ice-cold water until there is about 1 cup in the bowl). Pour it into the flour, stirring with a fork into a rough floury mass; never knead it. Turn it out in half-consistent state (divide into halves) onto the board. Roll out, fold back, and roll once, twice, and thrice. If properly made, it will be cold and hard to roll. (Put into refrigerator for 5–10 minutes if dough starts to get warm.) If necessary, use a little more flour. The butter will show in flakes as if not well mixed. It is safe, but if it is warm and shows a smooth greasy dough, it is a ruined pastry. Roll the piecrust thin; fill and cover; cut the 2 edges off with a knife; and press lightly.

Cheese Tarts

Glessner Family Recipe

1 package Philadelphia Cream Cheese
¼ pound butter
1 cup flour
Jam (any flavor)

Mix cream cheese, butter, and flour as you would a piecrust. Roll out and cut into 3-inch squares. Chill dough for about ½ hour. Put ½ teaspoon jam on each 3-inch square and fold over. Bake in quick oven at 375

three, and are surprised that their pies are tough or greasy and indigestible. These essentials are: ice-cold materials, hottest of ovens, and delicate manipulation. The oven can hardly be too hot. It should cook a pie in less than ten minutes. The pastry should be made in a cool place; never in a hot kitchen. Flour, board and rolling pin should all be cool. The butter should be ice-cold. When a cook takes the butter in her large warm hands and rubs it to a salve, then greases the flour with it, the pastry is ruined in the beginning."

degrees for 12–15 minutes or until crisp. Sprinkle with powdered sugar (optional).

Modern Cooking Tip: In selecting jam for this recipe, be sure *not* to use a seedless variety.

Banbury Tarts

PASTRY

Makes about 3 dozen tarts.
2 heaping cups flour, sifted
2 quarter pounds butter, minus 1 dinner square cup of each (14 tablespoons butter)
7 tablespoons cold water
1 teaspoon salt

Chop butter, flour, and salt till perfectly mixed. Add water. Stir with knife (cutting in ingredients). Pack down in a bowl. Put in icebox till next day.

Modern Cooking Tip: For preparation in a food processor: Chill flour and water. Cut butter into tablespoons and put aside and refrigerate. Combine flour and salt in bowl of food processor fitted with metal blade. Pulse on and off to mix. Distribute butter pats in bowl. Pulse until the consistency of fine crumbs. Drizzle water through feed tube 1 tablespoon at a time until mixture just begins to blend (cling together). All water may not be needed. Remove from food processor and blend by hand until dough sticks together to form a ball. Flatten into a disk and place on wax paper, refrigerate overnight. The next day, roll about between 2 layers of wax paper. Line a 9-inch tart tin without stretching dough.

FILLING
6 large figs (dried)
1 cup large seeded raisins
Rind and juice of 1 lemon (about 1 tablespoon grated rind and ¼ cup juice)

The Glessner family had an international day during one of their many visits to the exciting World's Columbian Exposition. They rode the great Ferris wheel, the first of its kind in the world, visited the Bedoin village, lunched at the German village, and sailed around the Liberal Arts Building. Their day ended at a concert, "where Lloyd sang most beautifully," recalled Mrs. Glessner.

Coming from a poetic family, Mr. Glessner wrote the following ode to the Christmas pie:

Dear Christmas pie
The pie's the thing
It's praises I sing
All you and I.

1 cup sugar
1 tablespoon water
1 teaspoon flour

Put through food processor. Work together with hands.

Modern Cooking Tip: Filling ingredients may be blended in a food processor. First pulse on and off, then process continuously until well blended. To bake: Spread processed ingredients in tart shell. Place in a 425-degree oven for 10 minutes and continue to bake at 325 degrees for 25 minutes, or until crust is golden brown and filling sets.

Lemon Chiffon Pie

Shortall Family Recipe

1 tablespoon (1 packet) unflavored gelatin
½ cup water
Juice of 1 lemon (¼ cup)
5 eggs, separated
1 cup sugar (½ reserved)
1 9-inch pie shell (see recipe, p. 157, or use commercially prepared shell)
3 tablespoons whipping cream (optional)

(Dissolve gelatin in water and set aside. Mix lemon juice, egg yolks, and ½ cup sugar well.) Cook in double boiler until thickened. Add dissolved gelatin. (Remove from heat and let cool.) Beat whites; add (reserved) sugar. Fold the mixture above into the whites. Put in a (baked) pastry shell in the icebox (chill to set). Crisscross with whipped cream.

The Stanley Field family's lemon pie recipe, known as "Buck's Lemon Pie," called for so much brandy that it was hazardous even after the cook had greatly reduced the liquor content. Katherine Field Rodman claimed that she "was drunk as a billy goat on one piece."

Famed minister Henry Ward Beecher seems to have forgotten that he was not in the pulpit when he wrote this following praise to the apple pie: "Some people think any apples will do for pies. But the best for eating is the best for cooking. Who would put into a pie any apple but the Spitzenburgh . . . It will accept almost every flavor of every spice, and yet nothing is so fatal to the rare and higher graces of apple pie as inconsiderate and vulgar spicing. It is not meant to be a mere vehicle for the exhibit of these spices in their own natures. It is a glorious unity in which sugar gives up its nature as sugar, and butter ceases to be butter and each flavorsome spice gladly vanishes from its own full nature, that all of them by a common death, may rise into the new life of an apple pie. Not that apple is longer apple. It too is transformed, and the final pie, though born of apple, sugar, butter, nutmeg, cinnamon and lemon, is like none of these, but the compound ideal of them all, refined, purified and by fire fixed in blissful perfection."

Apple Pie

5–7 apples sliced thin (about 5 cups)
½ cup sugar
½ teaspoon cinnamon
1 tablespoon lemon juice
Pinch of salt
½ teaspoon nutmeg
1 double 9-inch pie shell (see recipe, p. 157, or use commercially prepared shell)
2 tablespoons butter

Mix sugar, cinnamon, lemon juice, salt, and nutmeg. Pour over apples, mix, and place in layers in the shell. Dot apples with butter. Cover with crust and bake in hot oven (450 degrees) for 10 minutes; then in moderate oven (350 degrees) for about an hour.

Modern Cooking Tip: Mix apple slices and sugar mixture gently with hand or spoon in bowl until apples are well covered. Add more cinnamon and nutmeg to taste if spicier pie is desired.

Apple Custard Pie

1 cup milk
Yolks of 2 eggs (white reserved)
4 apples, grated
1 small spoon (teaspoon) melted butter
½ cup sugar
Nutmeg to flavor (⅛–¼ teaspoon)
Pinch of salt
1 9-inch pie shell (see recipe, p. 157, or use commercially prepared shell)
2 spoons (tablespoons) sugar

(Mix all ingredients together well and refrigerate until firm.) Bake in one crust (at 325 degrees for 25–30 minutes.) Make a meringue with whites of eggs and sugar (beat the egg whites to a stiff froth and add sugar delicately).

❧ Squash Pie

Makes 1 pie, serving 6.
1½ cups winter squash (2–3 acorn squashes)
½ cup brown sugar
1 teaspoon cinnamon
½ teaspoon ginger
½ teaspoon vanilla
1 teaspoon grated lemon rind
2 eggs
½ cup cream
1 9-inch pie shell (see recipe, p. 157, or use commercially prepared shell)

Remove seeds and bake squash until tender (pierce skin and bake, cut side down, in a 350-degree oven for 30–40 minutes, or until fork tender). Scrape and strain (through sieve). Mix squash with brown sugar, cinnamon, ginger, vanilla, and lemon rind. Add lightly beaten eggs. Then add cream. Fill shell. Bake in hot (400-degree) oven for 20 minutes. Finish baking in slow (325-degree) oven for 40 minutes.

Modern Cooking Tip: Squash can also be baked in a microwave oven. Prepare as above, put in 3-quart glass dish, cut side down, and cover with plastic wrap. Set on high for 13–16 minutes, and puree in a food processor.

When in Chicago, Edith Mason, the diva, was often entertained at the home of Arthur Meeker. She had such a passion for squash and mince pies, that when asked which she preferred she usually could not make up her mind and ate both.

Pies, made with a great variety of fillings, were a popular staple on Prairie Avenue. In the Bennett Harvey family, pies were often eaten at breakfast. The custom dates from Mr. Harvey's boyhood in Sandwich, Illinois, where the pie cupboard was well stocked at all times.

29. Box of Dr. Blumers High Grade
Flavoring Extracts, ca. 1910. From
the collection of the Glessner House
Museum.

Pudding

Charlotte Russe

Harvey Family Recipe

Makes 8–10 servings.
½ **pint (1 cup) milk**
½ **ounce unflavored gelatin**
1 **teacup (½ cup) sugar**
4 **eggs, separated**
1 **pint (2 cups) thick cream**
Vanilla to taste (about 1 teaspoon)
1 **good tablespoon brandy**
1 **sponge cake (see recipe, p. 154)**

To milk, put gelatin and sugar. Heat until gelatin has dissolved. Add the egg yolks beaten well together (over a low heat, stirring constantly until thick creamy yellow). Flavor with vanilla and brandy and cool. Beat cream very stiff, add to it the beaten whites of the eggs, and when the custard is cool, add that. Pour into mold (or springform pan) lined with slices of sponge cake to harden. (Chill until set.)

Modern Cooking Tip: Serve with pureed fresh raspberries spread over the top.

The regal charlotte russe was one of the desserts served at the lavish dedication banquet for the World's Columbian Exposition, held in the famous Auditorium Building on October 12, 1892. Mayor Washburne and General Milnes were assisted with the evening's dedication ceremonies by Prairie Avenue's own George Pullman and Marshall Field.

There was a stroke of the practical joker in Mrs. Glessner, a fact that came out one April Fool's Day, when she set before her son, George, beautiful homemade chocolates—nicely packed with cotton.

Indian Pudding
Glessner Family Recipe

Serves 6.

½ cup molasses
Suet (or butter) the size of an egg (¼ cup), chopped fine
6 tablespoons Indian meal (yellow cornmeal), sifted
1 cup sugar
1 tablespoon ground ginger
Pinch of salt
1 teaspoon cinnamon
2 eggs, well beaten

Scald 1 quart (4 cups) milk, molasses, and suet. When the suet is melted, add cornmeal, stirring constantly to avoid lumping (until thickened). Then pour into (lightly greased) pudding dish. Add 1 pint (2 cups) of cold milk, sugar, ginger, a little salt, and a little cinnamon, and, the last thing, the well-beaten eggs. Bake in a slow oven (275 degrees) 3 hours.

Modern Cooking Tip: Butter may be substituted for suet.

Dating at least to 1691, Hasty Pudding is one of the earliest known American desserts, a mixture of cornmeal, milk, and molasses, also known as "cornmeal mush" and "Indian pudding." Surely the most spartan of desserts, by the end of the nineteenth century, mush was commercially produced in Chicago and sold in retail stores. Steam-

Baked Indian Pudding
Fisk-Harvey Family Recipe

Makes 8 servings.

1 quart (4 cups) milk
5 tablespoons cornmeal
1 cup molasses
½ cup sugar
½ cup raisins
Pinch of salt
½ teaspoon cinnamon
3 eggs, beaten very lightly

Boil milk (then turn off heat and mix in cornmeal, molasses, sugar, raisins, salt, and cinnamon.) Pour, with all the fixings, on the eggs. Bake (in lightly greased pudding dish) in rather slow oven (275 degrees) 2 hours.

Genoise Cream

Meeker Family Recipe

Makes 8 servings.

1 quart (4 cups) milk
1 tablespoon cornstarch
Butter the size of an egg (¼ cup)
Yolks of 6 eggs
3 tablespoons sugar
1 pint (2 cups) whipping cream, beaten to full whip
Ladyfingers to line 9-inch dish
1 cup broken pecans or almonds (½ reserved)

(Add 2 tablespoons of the milk to cornstarch to make a paste; add a little more milk until fluid, then combine with remainder of milk, and put into nonaluminum saucepan.) Boil with butter. (Reduce to simmer.) Beat the eggs, then stir them into the boiling milk (2 tablespoons at a time). Add sugar. When cold, add (gently fold in) whipped cream. Line a (9-inch springform) dish with split ladyfingers, dipped in (Marsala) wine to make them adhere to the dish (brush outside of ladyfingers, stick on sides, and crumble onto bottom). Mix pecans or almonds into the custard, then pour slowly into the dish and put (reserved) nuts on the top.

Modern Cooking Tip: Chill overnight for the best result.

cooked pans of cold mush were marked in five-cent blocks that could be re-heated and fried. It is doubt-ful that this precooked prod-uct would have appeared on Prairie Avenue tables; none-theless, Hasty Pudding, a poor cousin to its richer, more elegant relatives, had its place on the sideboards of the street: "Put a pint and a half of milk into a sauce-pan, add a pinch of salt, and when the milk is just boiling up, sprinkle some fine flour with the left hand and beat well with a fork in the right, to keep the flour from getting in lumps. Con-tinue until the pudding is like a stiff, thick batter, which it will be when about a half pound of flour is used. Let it boil 5 or 6 min-utes longer, beating it all the time; then turn it into a dish with 2 or 3 ounces of fresh butter and serve immedi-ately. Be sure the milk is quite boiling when the flour is first put in."

At the conclusion of Sunday night suppers in the Glessner House, at which dress was always formal, Mr. Glessner would ceremoniously peel an orange impaled on a fork, keeping the peel whole, and present it to the lady on his right, without spilling a spurt of juice. On one memorable occasion, he displayed his virtuosity by peeling in this manner a white grape.

Ambrosia

Makes 4 servings.

2 large peeled navel oranges
¼ cup sugar (confectioners')
1⅓ cups grated coconut
3 tablespoons sherry

Slice peeled oranges (thinly). Make alternate layers of orange slices, sugar, and grated coconut until a glass dish is filled, having grated coconut on top; now a little sherry may be poured over the top to run through the mixture. (Chill before serving.)

Cranberry Pudding

Anderson Family Recipe

Makes 8–10 servings.

⅓ cup butter
⅔ cup sugar
2 eggs, separated
2⅓ cups flour
2 teaspoons baking powder
½ teaspoon salt
⅓ cup milk
1 cup cranberries

Cream butter and sugar (with an electric mixer or by hand). Add well-beaten yolks. Mix flour, baking powder, and salt. Add to butter and sugar and egg yolks alternately with milk. Fold in stiffly beaten whites of eggs and then add cranberries. Turn into greased mold (2½-cup capacity or larger) and steam 2 hours (place on a wire rack in a 5-quart pot filled with boiling water up to the rack, covered, over a low flame). If steamed in individual cups, 1½ hours. Serve with ice cream.

Modern Cooking Tip: This is not a pudding as we

know it, but has a cakelike texture. For a lighter pudding, bake, rather than steam, the mixture as the recipe instructs.

⚜️ *Plum Pudding*

Shortall Family Recipe

Makes 8–12 servings.
½ **pound (4 cups) bread crumbs (dry)**
1 cup scalded milk
¼ **pound (½ cup) sugar**
4 eggs, separated
½ **pound (1⅓ cups) seeded raisins, cut up**
¼ **cup currants**
2 ounces finely cut citron (candied)
½ **pound kidney suet, chopped**
¼ **cup brandy or mixed wine and brandy**
½ **nutmeg, grated (about 1 teaspoon ground nutmeg)**
¾ **teaspoon cinnamon**
⅛ **teaspoon ground cloves**
⅛ **teaspoon mace**
1½ **teaspoon salt**

Soak crumbs in (scalded) milk. Cool. Add sugar, beaten yolks, raisins, currants, citron, suet. Cream this by hand. Add spices, whites beaten stiff, and brandy. Steam 3 to 4 hours in buttered mold (2-quart, tightly covered. Place on rack over 2 inches boiling water in a 5-quart or larger kettle.)

Modern Cooking Tip: This is not a creamy pudding as we know it, but has a cakelike texture. For a lighter pudding, bake, rather than steam, the mixture as the directions instruct.

One enthusiastic cookbook described the many possibilities of bread crumbs: "Good bread will make good bread-crumbs . . . with poor bread have nothing to do. Toast gets to be an old story, so the next expedient is bread crumbs. Given a nice plate-ful of bread too dry for the table, put into the warming-oven till dry as powder, then crush very fine with rolling pin or potato masher, and you have the nucleus of a va-riety of dainty acceptable dishes. The crumbs can be prepared any time and kept in a tight, dry box or can. They will make first-class stuffing for turkeys and fowls, and a most desirable ingredient for plum or fruit puddings. . . . The half has not been told of the re-sources of bread crumbs, but lest you might weary of them, I'll only whisper in your ear, DON'T forget the "BREAD-CRUMBS."

Lemon Rice Pudding

Makes 6–8 servings.
2 teacups rice (1 cup long-grain rice)
1 pint (2 cups) water
1 quart new milk (4 cups whole milk)
3 eggs, separated
12 tablespoons sugar (¾ cup, half reserved)
Rind of 1 lemon (1 tablespoon, grated)
Juice of 1 lemon (¼ cup)

Boil rice till dry (bring to a boil and then simmer, covered, for about 18 minutes, until all the water is gone). Add milk and boil till thick (slow boil for about 25 minutes). Then add the egg yolks, well beaten, half of the sugar, and the rind of a lemon. Beat together and put in a pudding dish (or 10-inch diameter, 3-inch deep casserole dish). Beat the egg whites to a stiff froth, then add remaining sugar and the juice of a lemon. Spread it on the pudding and put it in the oven to brown (400 degrees for about 10 minutes).

Caramel Whip

Shortall Family Recipe

Makes 2 dozen.
1 tablespoon (1 envelope) gelatin
¼ cup cold water
1½ cups sugar
1 cup boiling water
5 eggs, separated
Whipped cream to top (optional)

Soften gelatin in the cold water (and set aside). Melt sugar (heat over very low heat, stirring constantly, for about 8–10 minutes) until caramelized (mixture will be the color of caramel). Then add boiling water and add to well-beaten egg yolks. Cook in a double boiler until thickened. Add gelatin to caramel mixture and cool. When syrupy, fold in stiffly beaten whites and put in dish in which it is to be served. Serve very cold with whipped cream. May also be made with maple syrup, cooked till it thickens.

Modern Cooking Tip: Caramelized sugar should be removed from the heat before the addition of boiling water, which should be made very slowly and carefully as the combination if added too quickly can be explosive. Add 1 or 2 tablespoons of the caramelized water to the egg yolks before pouring in the rest, so as to warm them and prevent curdling.

Apple Snow

We include this popular turn-of-the-century recipe, which is still a modern-day favorite, with the caveat that many nutritionists now caution against eating raw egg whites.

Makes 8 1-cup servings.
12 tart apples (5–6 pounds)
Whites of 12 eggs
½ pound (about 1½ cups) powdered sugar

Core, slice, and peel apples, put in cold water to cover. Cook over a slow fire (boil in a heavy-bottomed skillet, uncovered, as you would potatoes). When soft, drain and lay in deep dish. Add powdered sugar to apples. Beat to a froth. Beat egg whites stiff. Add and fold (apple mixture into) beaten egg whites. Beat whole to a stiff snow (holds its shape when spooned out). Turn into a dessert dish (or individual cups).

Modern Cooking Tip: 8 cups of natural, unsweetened applesauce may be substituted for the apples.

Lest they forget themselves, readers of American Etiquette and Rules of Politeness *were reminded in 1882, "Never pick your teeth, clean your nails, scratch your head or pick your nose in company."*

Afterthought Pudding

Makes 6 servings.

1 pint (2 cups) applesauce
2 eggs, separated
½ cups confectioners' sugar

To applesauce, sweetened to taste, add the beaten egg yolks and beat. Place in buttered dish, (deep-sided square 9-inch casserole) and bake 10–15 minutes (at 325 degrees). Then beat whites of eggs stiffly. Add sugar. Spread the meringue on top. Return to the oven till browned (another 10–15 minutes).

Sunday Pudding

Anderson Family Recipe

Makes 9 servings.

½ cup butter
1 cup sugar
1 cup milk
1 cup seeded raisins, cut small
3 tablespoons walnut meats
2 eggs, separated
2 cups flour
2 teaspoons baking powder
Spices (½ teaspoon each: ground ginger, clove, and nutmeg)
Pinch of salt

Steam in buttered cups for 45 minutes. (Pour into 3-inch buttered ramekins, ¾ full, and place in baking pan filled with ¼–½ inch water. Bake pan with ramekins on it in 350-degree oven. Remove and place on cooling rack.)

Modern Cooking Tip: To prepare for steaming: Cream butter and sugar by hand or with an electric mixer. Add milk, raisins, walnuts, and beaten egg

yolks; sift in flour, baking powder, spices, and salt.
Beat egg whites to a stiff peak and fold in.

SAUCE
1 cup sugar (confectioners')
½ cup butter
2 eggs, separated
**2 tablespoons wine, 1 tablespoon brandy, or 1
tablespoon vanilla**

(Beat butter until soft. Sift in sugar and blend well;
add egg yolks.) Cook in double boiler until thick and
smooth. Pour hot on whites beaten stiff. Add wine,
brandy, or vanilla. (Serve hot.)

30. Horse-drawn carriage in front of the William Hibbard home, 1638 Prairie Avenue.

Calling

By the 1860s the practice of "calling" was much in vogue. This ritual was governed by endless rules of etiquette spelled out in countless manuals dictating who was to call on whom and when, how soon return calls were expected, and how gentlemen callers were to proceed. "Leaving cards is one of the most important of social observances, as it is the groundwork or nucleus in society of all acquaintanceship," affirmed one such manual.

In a society as cultivated as that of Prairie Avenue, the rites of calling were not left to chance. *Bon Ton*, the official directory of the elite, listed families by name and by street and noted the day they were home to receive callers. Monday was Lake Shore Drive day, Tuesday South Side day, and Wednesday for the streets west of Lake Shore Drive. If there was a daughter of marriageable age, a small "dr." was added to the listing.

In polite society the task of leaving cards fell to the woman of a household, conspicuous evidence of her leisure time. "The fashionable time for leaving cards is between half past two and half past five o'clock," affirmed Silas Cobb in his manual, *The Use of Cards*. Cards were always to be delivered in person or by a servant, lest a mailed card suggest to the receiver that one had household responsibilities or other activity more highly valued.

Typically, a caller's carriage would pull up to a house, the coachman would alight with the visitor's card (right corner turned down if the caller was there in person), and deliver it to the front door. A married woman left her husband's card for the gentleman of the household as well as her own for his wife. Callers were not required to speak with the lady of the house; cards could be handed to a butler or maid, who would place them in a card receiver for the lady's later

31. Philip Armour parlor, 2115 Prairie Avenue, ca. 1890.

review. Should the caller wish to visit with the lady of the house, cards were placed on a silver tray and delivered by the servant to the employer, who would, in turn, indicate to her servant whether she was receiving visitors. Among social equals one was expected to reciprocate a card in return for a card, a call for a call. Between those of unequal social status different rules applied: a card returned with a call from a woman of higher social position was a great compliment; however, should the opposite occur, the caller was considered brash and presumptive.

For formal social events, written invitations were delivered by hand, frequently the coachman's. A common site on Prairie Avenue was that of the young Pullman twins enthusiastically assisting the coachman in his task—or undertaking it themselves by pony cart or bicycle. So sacred a trust were invitations that a columnist of the day commented that "if you died before the event took place, your hostess expected your executor to fill in for you." Scrupulously correct behavior required that dinner party invitees leave their calling card at the hostess's home after the engagement, whether or not one attended. It was suggested that this be carried out the day after the dinner, or at the very least within the week.

Calling became an exhausting ritual indeed, as Mrs. Glessner's journal indicates: "Friday I paid 12 calls . . . Monday I paid calls. Tuesday I received calls . . . I had 40 callers today." Upon leaving the city as an elderly widow, Mrs. George Pullman retired to a palatial railroad car, surrounded by her dogs. When asked if she didn't weary of traveling, Mrs. Pullman responded, "Oh no, indeed. I never get tired of traveling about in my own car all by myself, where there are no . . . front doorbells to disturb me, and no cards always being sent up. It's a great relief."

Calling ritual also protected the virtue of women, who were expected only to leave cards for other women. Mr. Cobb's manual spells out the rules of behavior for calling between the sexes in "Bachelors' Card Etiquette": "A gentleman may not call upon or leave his card for a married lady, or the mistress of a house, to whom he has been introduced, however gracious or agreeable she has been to him, unless she expressly asks him to call. . . . A gentleman may not under any circumstances leave a card on a lady to whom he has been introduced, unless her mother, chaperon, or the lady under whose care she is for the time, gives him the opportunity of furthering the acquaintance in the manner just indicated for married ladies. It

32. Marshall Field library, 1905 Prairie Avenue, ca. 1884.

would be considered 'ill-bred' were a gentleman to ask 'if he might have the pleasure of calling.'" However, a gentleman wishing to make the acquaintance of a young woman could arrange to have his card left at her home by a female friend. Should the young woman have no interest in meeting him, she would "not notice" his card. Servants could also be used as barriers to uninvited callers and announce that one was "not at home."

"Card leaving was a way of entering society, of designating changes in status or address, or issuing invitations and responding to them, of sending sentiments of happiness or condolence, and in general, of carrying on all the communication associated with social life," observed social historian Kenneth Ames. Changes in the home, workplace, and leisure time made this custom obsolete by the first decades of the twentieth century. Women became more culturally active, servant classes diminished, and suburbs spread, making it more difficult to frequently visit other households. The invention of the telephone finally diminished the need for personal calls. Today telephone calls have become our calling cards, and secretaries and answering machines the servants who announce that we are not available.

Victorian ceremony surrounding activities of daily life was perceived of as a means to achieve elegance and personal nobility. Beneath the veneer of propriety, however, a sense of humor could prevail, sufficient to allow Mrs. Glessner to respond to a note of invitation: "Thank you, thank you Charlotte dear/ For your kind invitation./ At two o'clock pray have no fear/ You'll find me at my station."

33. Nannie Scott (Mrs. Marshall) Field and children Marshall Field, Jr., and Ethel.

Cookies
and Assorted
Desserts

Lemon Jumbles

Makes 4 dozen 2½-inch cookies.

½ cup butter
1 cup sugar
1 egg
1 large lemon, juice and rind (½ cup lemon juice,
2 tablespoons lemon rind)
3 teaspoons milk
1½ teaspoons baking powder
Enough flour to make a dough that can be rolled
out very thin (2½ cups)

Cut with a doughnut cutter or thimble, so that
jumbles will be in rings. Requires a hot oven.

Modern Cooking Tip: To prepare dough to be rolled
out and cut: Cream together butter and sugar with an
electric beater or by hand. Beat in egg, lemon juice,
and rind, then add milk and baking powder. Add flour
a cup at a time. Roll on wax paper and shape into a
ball or drop in spoonfuls onto a cookie sheet and
flatten each cookie with a fork. Refrigerate for 3–4
hours or freeze for 45 minutes. Best results are
achieved when jumbles are baked on a lightly greased
cookie sheet in a 375-degree oven for approximately
10 minutes, or until lightly browned on the edges.

*Jumbles, among the first
American cookies, came in
various shapes and sizes
and usually consisted of
nuts "jumbled" up in the
dough. They were prepared
in vast quantities on Prairie
Avenue, a bountifulness that
may have started years before when, according to lore,
young Lydia Beekman was
caught unprepared for sere-
naders who came calling.
The custom was to reward
the minstrels by lowering a
basket of cookies from a window. Having no cookies on
hand, Lydia improvised
with a pailful of pickles. The
ominous silence in which
they were received caused
her to go out early the next
morning, to find a pickle impaled on every picket of the
front fence.*

Vanities

When Mrs. Arthur Meeker traveled to the West, she usually carried a well-stocked picnic basket, insurance against the dining car food that she viewed skeptically. One of these trips Arthur Meeker, Jr., escorted her to the station to find that Henry James would be her fellow traveler. He introduced them with some trepidation, fearing Mrs. Meeker might find the famed author somewhat overpowering. But not so Mrs. Meeker, whose note arrived a week later exclaiming, "I had a delightful visit with your friend Mr. James, and he did seem so to enjoy my ginger cookies."

Makes about 3 dozen cookies.

1 large egg
1 tablespoon sugar
$\frac{1}{16}$ teaspoon salt
5 drops vanilla
2½ tablespoons water
1 cup flour, sifted very gradually
4 cups vegetable shortening
¼ cup confectioners' sugar

Beat a large egg well, stir in sugar, a speck of salt, and vanilla. Add water and stir in flour, sifted very gradually. Knead on the board until smooth; a very little more flour may be needed for rolling, but be sparing, as the dough must be rolled very thin. Roll as thin as ordinary pasteboard (about ⅛-inch thick—add a drop of water if necessary to thin pastry) and cut into strips 4 inches long and 1 inch wide. When all are cut, slit each down the center to within 1 inch of either end. Slip one end through this gash and give it a twisted appearance. Now hold both ends between the thumb and forefingers of each hand and let slip into hot fat (approximately ¼ inch of vegetable shortening in the bottom a heavy skillet). They must be watched and turned as soon as they begin to get brown, as they cook in a few minutes (about 1 minute per side). Drain and sift confectioners' sugar over them. This is a small portion and can be doubled if desired.

Modern Cooking Tip: Vanities can be cooked in a deep fryer; heat to 400 degrees.

Hermits

Glessner Family Recipe

Makes about 1½ dozen bar cookies.

3 cups flour
¼ teaspoon salt
¼ teaspoon nutmeg
½ teaspoon cinnamon
1 teaspoon soda
½ cup nutmeats (chopped coarse)
½ cup dates (chopped or diced)
1 orange rind grated
½ cup butter or shortening
1½ cup brown sugar
2 tablespoons sour milk
2 eggs (beaten well)

Cream together butter, sugar, and orange rind. Sift together flour, salt, nutmeg, cinnamon, and soda and set aside. Add beaten eggs to butter and sugar mixture. Alternate adding dry ingredients and sour milk, then fold in dates and nuts. Spoon into (greased and floured) 9-by-13-inch pan and bake at 350 degrees for 25–30 minutes. (Cut into bars when cool.)

Modern Cooking Tip: Sour milk can be fabricated by adding a few drops of lemon juice to milk.

Hard Ginger Cookies

Glessner Family Recipe

Makes about 2 dozen.

½ cup sugar
½ cup shortening
½ cup molasses
½ teaspoon ginger
½ teaspoon cinnamon

Hermits are chewy cookies with a cakelike consistency that are flavored with lots of spices. Legend traces their popularity to sailors on clipper ships in the mid-nineteenth century, who favored them because they kept well in canisters aboard ship on long sea voyages, providing variety to an otherwise monotonous diet.

½ teaspoon baking soda
¼ cup hot water
2 cups flour

Mix ingredients in order given: sugar, shortening, molasses, ginger, cinnamon, and flour, being sure to add enough flour so that dough handles easily for rolling. Dissolve baking soda in hot water. Roll dough and cut into shapes with cookie cutters. Bake in moderate oven (350–375 degrees) for 10–15 minutes.

 Drop Ginger Cakes

Makes 2 dozen cupcakes.

1 cup butter
1 teacup (½ cup) sugar
4 eggs
1 pint (2 cups) molasses
1 tablespoon baking soda, dissolved in ½ teacup (¼ cup) hot water
2 tablespoons ginger
2 tablespoons ground cinnamon
1 teaspoon salt
Flour enough to make batter (5 cups)

Drop (by the tablespoon) in lined (or lightly greased) muffin tins. Bake in moderate oven (350 degrees for 10–12 minutes, or until centers are firm to the touch).

Modern Cooking Tip: To prepare for baking: Cream butter and sugar with an electric mixer or by hand. Add eggs and beat until light and fluffy. Mix in molasses, baking soda in water, and remaining ingredients sifted together. Beat until smooth. Serve with lemon sauce (see recipe, p. 203).

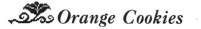 *Orange Cookies*

Makes 4 dozen.

2 tablespoons orange rind
4 tablespoons butter
1 cup sugar
2 eggs
4 tablespoons orange juice
2 cups sifted flour
4 teaspoons baking powder
½ teaspoon salt

Cream together the grated rind, butter, and sugar.
Add the well-beaten eggs and orange juice. Then add
the flour, baking powder, and salt, which have been
sifted together. Drop dough with teaspoon onto a
buttered cookie sheet and bake in moderate oven at
350 degrees for 10 minutes.

Ladyfingers

Makes 1½ to 2 dozen.

Whites of 7 or 8 eggs, according to size
6 ounces (¾ cup) powdered sugar
4 ounces (½ cup) flour (double sifted before
measuring)
1 rounded teaspoon cream of tartar
½ teaspoon lemon extract (optional)
Powdered sugar for dusting

Whip the whites to a perfectly firm froth (to form
peaks, but not dry). Have the sugar, flour, and cream
of tartar all well mixed together by running through a
sieve (sifted); add them and the lemon extract, to
flavor, to the whites and stir without beating (folding
gently) till fairly mixed.

Fill the ladyfinger sack and tube with the mixture
(or use a paper funnel); press out finger shapes onto a
sheet of paper; sift powdered sugar over plentifully.

Catch up 2 corners of the paper, shake off the loose sugar, put the sheet on a baking pan, and bake in a slack oven (325 degrees for 15–18 minutes, or until light and golden all over). Dampen the paper, underside, with a brush dipped in water, to get the cakes off (or use a spatula). This mixture may also be baked in molds.

Modern Cooking Tip: A pastry tube or cookie press may be substituted for the lady finger sack and tube or paper funnel.

 ## Chocolate Cookies

Glessner Family Recipe

For special family dinners, seating at the Hibbard residence was by age, with the youngest at the foot of the table. Gold Hibbard II, well into adolescence at the time, complained, "I never get past the middle of the table."

1 cup brown sugar sifted
½ cup butter
Pinch of salt
1 egg
½ cup milk
1½ cups flour
1 teaspoon baking soda
1 heaping teaspoon baking powder
1½ squares unsweetened chocolate—melted
1 teaspoon vanilla
½ cup chopped walnuts

Mix butter, brown sugar, milk, and vanilla. Then add egg and beat mixture. In a separate bowl mix flour, salt, and baking soda and baking powder. Fold dry ingredients into batter. Then add melted chocolate. And finally fold in chopped nuts. Bake at 325 degrees for 15 minutes.

Modern Cooking Tip: Sprinkle cookies with powdered sugar or frost with chocolate frosting, placing a ½ walnut on top.

Grandma Cookies

Keith Family Recipe

This recipe uses less flour than those for the modern oatmeal cookies we are used to, creating a thinner, lacier cookie.

Makes about 5½ dozen.

2¼ cups rolled oats
3 tablespoons flour
Pinch of salt
2¼ cups brown sugar (light)
½ pound (1 cup) melted butter
1 egg, slightly beaten
1½ teaspoons vanilla

Put rolled oats, flour, salt, and sugar in bowl and stir. Melt butter and let it get hot, not bubbly. Stir into the mixture till sugar is melted. Add egg and vanilla. Place small teaspoonfuls 2 inches apart on greased cookie sheet. Cook 7 minutes in 375-degree oven. Let cool slightly to harden before removing from cookie sheet.

Modern Cooking Tip: The cookie sheet needs to be greased even if a teflon or nonstick surface is used. These cookies will spread much more than flour-based cookies.

Keith descendants fondly recall a favorite coachman whose dedication to his work was so strong that he, marrying late in life, sent his young bride alone to Kentucky for the honeymoon.

Fudge Brownies

Glessner Family Recipe

Makes 25–30.

4 squares of unsweetened chocolate—melted
½ pound butter
4 eggs—beaten
2 cups sugar

Brownies were a late nineteenth-century concoction: the term first appeared in print in the 1897 Sears, Roebuck and Company catalog.

1 cup flour
1½ cup chopped walnuts
2 teaspoon vanilla

Mix sugar, vanilla, and eggs. To this add butter and chocolate melted together (in double boiler). Fold in flour. Then add nuts. Pour into buttered pan (9-by-12 inches). Bake for 35 minutes at 375 degrees. Cool before cutting.

 ## Genuine Scotch Shortbread

A note accompanying this recipe proclaims that "it makes the most delicious shortbread ever eaten in this country."

Makes about 5–6 dozen cookies.

1 pound (2 cups) butter
1 cup sugar
4 cups flour

Rub butter and sugar together to a cream. The flour should be dry and slightly warm. Mix into the butter and sugar gently with the hand until all ingredients are thoroughly incorporated. The longer it is kneaded, the better it will be. Lay it on a floured pastry board and press into sheets nearly ½-inch thick with the hand, as rolling has a tendency to toughen it. Cut into shapes as desired; prick or stamp a pattern on top. Sometimes the Scotch thistle is pricked upon it. Bake (on a cookie sheet) in a moderate oven until it is crisp and of a fine yellow brown (325 degrees for 25–30 minutes).

Delicate Gingerbread

Mrs. William Vaughn Moody, wife of the poet, launched the successful catering service Home Delicacies by using a version of this recipe to bake individual gingerbread for Marshall Field's department store.

Makes 1 loaf.

⅔ cup butter
2 cups molasses
1 tablespoon baking soda
1 tablespoon cinnamon
1 tablespoon ginger

1 grated nutmeg (1 teaspoon)
1 cup sour milk (buttermilk)
1 egg, beaten
3 cups flour, measured before sifting

Heat the butter with the molasses over the fire (in a heavy 3-quart saucepan). When it comes to the boil, stir in the soda and the spices. Remove from the stove and put in the milk and the egg thoroughly beaten. Beat all well. Then beat in the sifted flour. Bake in individual pans (or in 1 large pan, about 13 by 9 by 2 inches). Bake in a rather quick oven (375 degrees) for approximately 20–30 minutes (or until tester comes out clean or cake comes away from the sides of the pan).

Gingerbread

Meeker Family Recipe

Makes 1 loaf.
½ cup butter
½ cup sugar
¾ cup molasses (blackstrap)
1 teaspoon baking soda
1 teaspoon ginger
2 teaspoons cinnamon
⅛ teaspoon nutmeg
½ cup sweet (whole) milk
2 eggs, well beaten
2½ cups flour

Modern Cooking Tip: As no directions survived with these ingredients, the following cooking steps are recommended: Beat butter and sugar well together. Heat with molasses. When it comes to a boil, stir in soda, ginger, cinnamon, and nutmeg. Remove from the stove and add milk and eggs, well beaten. Beat in flour thoroughly. Bake in a 9-inch lightly greased loaf

At weekday lunches with Arthur Meeker's grandmother, no parents were allowed. The menu might be creamed beef, scalloped tomatoes braced with sugar, and, for dessert, gingerbread or Indian pudding.

pan in a preheated 375-degree oven for 20–30 minutes, or until tester comes out clean or cake comes away from the sides of the pan(s).

Omelette au Rhum
Shortall Family Recipe

Makes 4 servings.

5 eggs, separated
1⅓ tablespoons powdered sugar (plus additional
¼–⅓ cup to top)
Pinch of salt
5 tablespoons butter (4 tablespoons reserved)
Rum to flame (about ¼ cup)

Beat egg yolks with 1⅓ tablespoons powdered sugar. Beat whites separately with pinch of salt. Turn yolks into whites, beat together, adding in bits about a level tablespoon butter. (Melt remaining butter in a very hot skillet but do not burn. Add egg mixture and cook over a medium flame.) Cook till not quite done (slightly runny on top). Remove without folding to platter; cover thickly with powdered sugar, pour rum over, and set fire. Send blazing to table.

Modern Cooking Tip: Rum should be heated, as should the platter, in order to get a successful flame. Pour most of the rum around, rather than in the middle, of the omelette for ease in flaming. This yields a very fluffy omelette, the sweetest of desserts!

Candy

During candymaking sessions in the Glessner household, furniture was pushed against the walls to make room for alcohol pressure stoves, white enamel kettles, long candy thermometers,

Children's parties are high on the list of Prairie Avenue memories, and there were plenty of them: candy-pulling parties, doll parties, whooping cough parties, sleigh rides, and the marvelous Punch and Judy shows of Professor Singleton. This simple and traditional recipe for candy drops can be prepared with children in almost any flavor by altering the extract flavoring.

2 cups sugar
1 cup water
Lemon or peppermint extract

Boil till sugar cracks when dropped in water (or sugar breaks when a wet object is dipped into boiling sugar and back again into cold water), flavor with a few drops of lemon or peppermint; drop in small drops on buttered (wax) paper. (Paper must be buttered or candy drops will stick to it.)

Nougat

½ cup powdered sugar
Caramel (1 14-ounce bag wrapped candies)
½ cup almonds, chopped
1½ teaspoons glucose (Karo Syrup)

Melt powdered sugar into caramel, add chopped almonds and a teaspoon and a half of glucose. Roll out on marble slab (or cookie sheet) well greased with oil.

Modern Cooking Tip: Nuts can be chopped in a Cuisinart by pulsating the on-and-off switch or in a coffee grinder by grinding for a few seconds until desired size is reached.

wooden stirring paddles, and children. They made chocolate creams, caramels, fudge, and peanut brittle, but the most fun of all was taffy. One year, professional equipment purchased to simplify taffymaking provided its own amusement. John Glessner Lee recalled candy fed into the machine flying all over the room, banging into windows 15 feet away, bouncing off the ceiling, careening across the floor, hopping into chairs, and ricocheting off mirrors. When the cranking stopped, the room was hopelessly stuck, and for days candy was found in bed mattresses and curtains.

Prairie Avenue children delighted when mother's shopping trip included a stop at Madam Mary's candy store in the Auditorium Building to buy the best nougat candy available in Chicago. Madam Mary's famous nougat came in 8-inch squares so hard they had to be broken with a hammer or dropped on the hearth.

34. Ice-cream truck in front of George Pullman's carriage house and the Fort Dearborn Massacre Monument on Eighteenth Street and Prairie Avenue.

Ice Creams, Sorbet, and Dessert Sauces

The art of making iced desserts was in full swing by the mid-nineteenth century, spurred on by the patenting in 1848 of the crank ice-cream maker, Johnson's Patent Ice Cream Freezer. *Godey's Lady's Book* of 1850 commented that "ice cream had become one of the necessities of life. A party without it would be like a breakfast without bread or a dinner without a roast." A newspaper clipping from the scrapbook of Prairie Avenue resident Mrs. D. B. Fisk elaborates on the pleasures of ice cream: "A plate of ice cream taken leisurely, while seated at a table in pleasurable conversation is a far safer quencher of thirst than a glass of ice water, or any other ice-cold liquid; the ice cream is, in addition, stimulating and nutritious, thus invigorating, cooling and strengthening the system at the same time." By the end of the century Americans ate five million gallons of ice cream a year.

Harper's Cookbook Encyclopedia described the variety among iced treats:

- Water ices are made of the juices of ripe fruits mixed with syrup and frozen, and it must be remembered that if the juices are sweetened excessively they will not freeze.
- French Ice-Creams are based on custards made of scalded milk and the yolks of eggs, and stirred while freezing.
- Mousses, Biscuits and Parfaits are made of whipped cream, which is frozen without stirring.

- American Ice-Creams are made of cream (or milk) and sugar, flavored by extracts or by fruits, and stirred while freezing.
- Punches and Sherbets are water ices to which liquors have been added.

The ice-cream sundae is purported to be the creation of Chicago's outlying village of Evanston, Illinois. Civic moralists there denounced "the Sunday soda menace" and enacted legislation to prohibit drinking soda water on the Sabbath. Creative vendors simply formed a new dessert that would not threaten public morals, replacing the offending soda with ice cream covered with flavored syrups or toppings, which they dubbed "ice-cream sundae." The fad was secured when the Women's Christian Temperance Union heralded the new dessert as an alternative to alcohol.

Ice-cream concoctions soon became quite elaborate. A Chicago newspaper described with wonder the ice-cream desserts served at the Kinsley's dinner party: "The ice cream came to the table in the form of asparagus stalks and bananas. Cakes filled with ice cream were made to take the form and appearance of baked potatoes, and the deception was so perfect as to excite the wonder and admiration of all present." An 1897 issue of *American Kitchen Magazine* contained an article entitled "Frozen Jewels," encouraging enterprising hostesses to serve "ice cream gems. . . . a slice of flashing ruby or . . . a spoonful of emeralds." The following two recipes from *The Cookbook of "Oscar of the Waldorf"* evidence how complex the making and presentation of ice-cream desserts had become.

 ## Nougat Ice Cream

"Put the nougat in a mortar with two tablespoonfuls of orange-flower water, and pound it. Put the yolks of three eggs in a saucepan with one and one-half pints of cream, and twelve tablespoonfuls of fine sugar and beat. Mix the bruised nougat and three drops of the essence of peach kernels with the milk and eggs, and stir the whole over the fire till on the point of thickening. Pass the mixture through a fine hair-sieve into the basin and leave until cooled. When ready turn the nougat cream into the freezer and freeze it. The cream can be served as it is or may be turned into moulds and packed in ice for about two hours. Before serving, the mould should be dipped in warm water, wiped, and the contents turned out on a fancy dish."

Carnot Sherbet

"Have in readiness an orange water ice, in which mix a little carmine [red food coloring], kirsch and orange-flower water. It should be dressed in a small nest with a little bird perched on its edge; the bird, the inside and the bottom should be made of gum paste, and the outside of the nest should be imitated with spun sugar and the grass with fillets of angelica. It should be served immediately on its completion."

MODERN COOKING TIPS
FOR ICE CREAMS

Some explanation is advisable to assist the reader with these ice-cream recipes. First of all, most of these recipes require heavy cream, or whipping cream (*not* cream that has been prewhipped, however). Some recipes use thin cream, which is the equivalent of the contemporary commercial product Half & Half.

Although these recipes will work well if made in an ice cream maker, they do not require one. They can be made with equal success utilizing one of two Victorian methods of making ice cream that do not require an ice-cream maker. One method is as follows: the fruit or flavored components of the ice cream (everything minus eggs and cream), which are frozen first, usually overnight. This mixture is then removed from the freezer, and cream, beaten to a full whip, and eggs (if called for) are added, and the whole mixture is again frozen to yield the finished ice cream. This method worked very well for us in every instance, however we caution that your freezer must be very cold: approximately 5 degrees Fahrenheit ($\pm$ 5 degrees).

In some instances the two-step freezing process was not necessary, as has been indicated in the instructions with each recipe. In these cases, simply beat the cream to a whipped constituency, stir into it the flavoring components of the ice cream, and freeze this mixture at once. It is important that heavy cream be very cold when it is beaten into a whip, and that this be done in a cold bowl with chilled utensils in order not to sacrifice thickness and creaminess of the finished ice cream. Ice creams made in this manner were very creamy in texture and did not require an ice-cream maker. Should an ice cream be yielded that is too crystalline with ice when it is done, the texture can be improved by removing it from the freezer, thawing it just enough to stir it thoroughly, then reinserting it into the freezer. This should replace the icy texture with a creamy, smooth one.

Vanilla Ice Cream

Makes 1 pint of ice cream.
2 cups cream (whipping cream)
1 egg
1 cup sugar
⅛ teaspoon vanilla

One pint of cream, one egg, one cup of sugar; egg beaten separately, sugar in the yolk, then beaten very hard together, stir the eggs into the cream; flavor with vanilla. Freeze.

Modern Cooking Tip: In other words, separate yolk and egg whites into separate bowls. Add sugar to the yolk mixture and mix well. Beat egg white and pour into yolk mixture, beat hard. Freeze in chilled ceramic

The following newspaper clipping was found in the scrapbook of Mrs. D. B. Fisk, grandmother of Bennett Harvey: "Ice cream should not be taken immediately after a full meal, unless in the most leisurely manner possible, a plate full in the course of 15 minutes during lively conversation. If eaten rapidly, it cools the stomach, prevents digestion, and causes acidity, unseemly belching, if not actual chill, which in feeble persons endangers life."

bowl that has been in freezer for an hour. Remove from freezer and blend cream into mixture, then add vanilla and refreeze. A commercial ice-cream maker can also be used in place of the frozen bowl and successive freezing method described above.

Chocolate Ice Cream

Makes 1 pint ice cream.
2 squares semisweet chocolate
¼ cup sugar
½ cup cold milk
1 egg
¼ cup thin cream (Half & Half)
¼ tablespoon vanilla
¼ tablespoon brandy

Put chocolate in double boiler, add cold milk, and cook over hot water until thick and smooth; the time required being about 7–10 minutes. Let cool, beat egg, and add ¼ cup sugar; then add 1 cup thin cream. Add 1 tablespoon each vanilla and brandy and beat hard. Combine with chocolate mixture and freeze hard.

Modern Cooking Tip: Chill ceramic bowl in freezer for about an hour. A commercial ice cream maker can also be used in place of the frozen bowl and successive freezing method described above.

Lemon Ice Cream

Makes 1 pint of ice cream.
Rind of 2 lemons (½–¾ cup, grated)
Juice of 1 lemon (½ cup)
¾ cup sugar
1 pint thick cream (whipping cream)

Rasp the yellow rind of 2 large, fresh lemons upon pounded (granulated) sugar. Strain over it the juice of

The May 1889 Ladies Home Journal *suggested hosting a "Lemon Squeeze, . . . invite all your friends to bring a lemon without telling them why: They will wonder what for, and that is the beginning of the fun." Lemons are placed in a large basket, five have ribbons around them, and each guest draws one. Those picking beribboned lemons become the "Committee on Squeezing." Victims then march before this august committee to have their lemon squeezed and the number of seeds recorded, while lemonade accumulates in a nearby pitcher. When the last guest's lemon has been squeezed, everyone guesses the number of seeds in the bowl, and prizes are then awarded. The* Ladies Home Journal *suggested churches and charitable organizations host this "home frolic."*

On January 16, 1903, the Glessners served dinner to 96 members of the Chicago Symphony Orchestra; 26 were seated in the dining room, 24 in the library, 18 in the main hall, and 28 in the parlor. For this lavish affair they recruited 15 extra waiters, 1 headwaiter, 2 coachmen, 1 man to serve ice cream, 2 women to help with dishes, 2 others to help the cook, and 3 others to help set up during the day; all of these in addition to the regular household staff of 8!

At a dinner party held at the home of famous pianist Fannie Bloomfield Zeisler, guests and their hostess learned to their dismay that

1 lemon. Put in cold bowl and freeze hard. Whip cream and add to fruit mixture, mix and freeze.

Modern Cooking Tip: Chill ceramic bowl in freezer for about an hour. A commercial ice cream maker can also be used in place of the frozen bowl and successive freezing method described above.

 ## Orange Ice Cream

Glessner Family Recipe

Makes 1 pint of ice cream.

¾ **cup sugar**
¾ **cup water**
1½ **cup orange juice**
1 **tablespoon lemon juice**
1 **orange rind, grated**
½ **cups heavy cream (whipping cream)**
2 **egg whites**

Boil sugar and water 10 minutes. Add orange rind and boil a few minutes longer. Remove orange rind and add sugar mixture to lemon and orange juice. Pour into tray and freeze firm. Remove to ice-cold bowl and beat until light. Add heavy cream and fold in stiffly beaten egg whites. Freeze.

Modern Cooking Tip: Chill ceramic bowl in freezer for about an hour. A commercial ice-cream maker can also be used in place of the frozen bowl and successive freezing method described above.

Raspberry Cream Ice

Makes 1 pint of ice cream.

2–3 **pints fresh raspberries**
1½ **cup sugar**
1 **pint thick cream (whipping cream)**

Beat 1 pound of fresh raspberries through a hair sieve; mix pulp with pounded (granulated) sugar. Whip cream, add to fruit mixture, and freeze hard.

Modern Cooking Tip: Raspberries can be pulverized in a blender, then strained of seeds in a large, fine flat sieve. Removal of seeds is preferable for a finer texture, but not necessary; removal of half the seeds is advisable for an acceptable texture. Chill ceramic bowl in freezer for about an hour. Whipping cream can also be whipped until thick in a blender before adding to the raspberry mix and refreezing. A commercial ice cream maker can also be used in place of the frozen bowl and successive freezing method described above.

Peach Ice Cream

Makes 1 pint of ice cream.
1 dozen peaches, cut into small pieces
¾ cup sugar
1 pint thick cream

Cut in small pieces 1 dozen peaches, or more if desired, and boil them with loaf sugar (granulated sugar). When reduced to a marmalade, press them thoroughly through a fine sieve. Let cool about 1 hour, beat cream into mixture, and freeze hard. Serve with halves or quarters of fresh peaches half frozen around the cream.

Modern Cooking Tip: If texture is desired, eliminate straining of fruit mixture and puree in blender after reducing peach mixture to marmalade. Chill ceramic bowl in freezer for about an hour. A commercial ice-cream maker can also be used in place of the frozen bowl and successive freezing method described above.

their dessert course would have to be indefinitely delayed. Someone made off with the ice-cream freezer sitting on the back porch during their meal.

At a dinner held for novelist Miss Lilian Bell in 1893, small folded cards shaped like a book were placed in the ice cream at each place setting. The cards had been printed in elaborate calligraphy with the words "The Love Affairs of an Old Maid," the title of a popular short story written by the guest of honor.

"How many housekeepers
have received with dismay
the news that some intimate
friend is visiting a neighbor's in sultry, summer
weather, . . . when the thermometer is most at home in
the nineties, and even when
thoughts of food and dining
produce discomfort?" asked
Mrs. Garrett Webster in the
May 1894 issue of the La-
dies Home Journal. Her an-
swer—a refreshing Ice Dinner: "covering the table with
the snowiest of linen cloths,
and use for a centerpiece a
frosted-glass bowl of white,
or so-called Christmas,
roses. At each cover place a
guest card of pure white
pasteboard sprinkled with di-
amond dust, in imitation of
frost . . . having tied to it a
bunch of white roses." She
suggested a simple menu:
oysters on the half shell
served on cracked ice, celery,
no soup, cold trout or
salmon, a salad course of
Neufchâtel cheese, and dessert of vanilla ice cream
"molded into snow-balls,
and ornamented with a
sprig of holly or evergreen,"
served with any white-iced
cake, followed by iced coffee
and white bonbons.

Grape Ice Cream

Makes 1 pint of ice cream.

⅔ cup grape juice (⅓ cup grape juice concentrate,
⅓ cup water to dilute)
1 cup thick cream
1 tablespoon lemon juice
Sugar enough to sweeten (½ cup)
¼ cup pistachio nuts, chopped

Stir 1 cup grape juice into a pint of thick cream; add 1
tablespoon of lemon juice and sugar enough to
sweeten; whip until thick and pour into a mold; freeze.
Garnish with a fine sprinkling of pistachio nuts.

Modern Cooking Tip: Fresh grapes can be
substituted for grape juice for an equally enjoyable ice
cream. If this is done, use ½ pound (or 1 cup) of
seedless grapes, peeled, and pureed in a blender.

Banana Sherbet

Makes 1½ pints sherbet.

1 cup sugar
2 cups water
Juice of 1 small lemon
Juice of 1 orange
½ dozen bananas, mashed fine
1 cup cream (whipping)

Boil together for 5 minutes sugar and water, let cool,
then add the juice of a small lemon and 1 orange and
½ dozen bananas mashed fine. Freeze in ice-cold bowl
until hard. Remove from freezer, then pour in 1 cup
cream and freeze hard. Serve in punch cups.

 ## Regents Punch

Glessner Family Recipe

Makes about 2 quarts.

1 pound loaf sugar or rock candy
1 large cup strong black tea
3 wineglasses brandy
3 wineglasses rum
1 bottle champagne
Juice of 2 oranges
Juice of 3 lemons
1 large lump of ice

Mix and serve.

While visiting Prairie Avenue during the World's Columbian Exposition, Mrs. Frederick Law Olmsted informed her hostess that she took no chances on her travels around the country. She always carried in her bag two bottles, one filled with bicarbonate of soda and the other with alcohol, labeled respectively "Sweetness" and "Light."

Roman Punch

Glessner Family Recipe

Makes about 2 quarts.

3 coffee cups (3 cups) lemonade (strong and sweet)
1 glass champagne
1 glass rum
Juice of 2 oranges
2 egg whites (well whipped)
½ pound pulverized sugar (granulated sugar)

(In a large bowl) beat sugar into the stiffened egg whites. Add lemonade, champagne, rum, and orange juice. Ice abundantly or freeze.

Newspapers exuberantly recounted the dinner party given in honor of "the charming writer" Miss Lilian Bell, at the home of Mr. and Mrs. Orr in 1893. They reported: "the home of the host and hostess was decorated with a profusion of flowers and palms, and Mrs. Orr received in a gown of satin duchesse trimmed with lace . . . Miss Bell read from her short stories, and Mrs. E. R. Sharpe, Misses Spencer, Kohlsaat and Lamson served frappe."

On informal social occasions, there were musicians and refreshments throughout the Glessners' house, and merriment marked the evening: Beethoven was rendered on spoons, pots, pans, sieves, bottles, and glasses filled with water to various levels. Guests even tried the impossible stunt of picking a card up off the floor with their teeth while balancing a bottle of champagne on their head. Years later it was rumored that an overstimulated guest once forgot himself and "pinched the ladies." But no hint of such behavior ever reached the ear of his decorous hostess.

At her afternoon musicales, Mrs. George Pullman served a Roman punch that was not for the meek. When approached by a guest with a comment on the strength of the brew, Mrs. Pullman retorted, "Well, hell, we're pioneers!"

Romaine Punch

Palmer Family Recipe

Serves 8–10.

4½ cups water (½ cup reserved)
2½ cups sugar (½ cup reserved)
Juice of 6 good-size lemons (2–2½ cups)
Juice of 1 orange (½–¾ cups)
Whites of 4 eggs
1 gill (½ cup) sherry
2 tablespoons Jamaica rum

Boil together a quart (4 cups) of water and a pint (2 cups) of sugar for about ½ hour; add lemon juice and orange juice; strain and set away to cool. Then prepare the following: Boil together a gill (½ cup) of sugar and a gill of water for 18 minutes. While the syrup is cooking, beat the egg whites very stiff and into these pour the hot syrup very slowly—beating all the time, and continue to beat a few minutes after it is all in. Set this away to cool.

Place the first mixture in the freezer and freeze by turning it all the time for 20 minutes. Then take off the cover, remove the beater, and add sherry, rum, and the meringue, mixing this well with a spoon into the frozen preparation. Cover again and set away until time to serve. Serve in punch glasses as a course between entrees and roast.

This is a punch that "packs a wallop," as one former resident of Prairie Avenue recalled. Maestro Thomas, founding conductor of the Chicago Symphony Orchestra, enjoyed a passion for fine food and drink that made him a frequent dinner guest at the Prairie Avenue

Theodore Thomas Punch

Serves 4–6.

¼ Burgundy
¼ Moselle (a light, Rhine wine)
½ champagne

These fractions are proportions to be used in mixing any quantity of this punch, rather than fractions of one wine bottle.

Brandy Sauce

½ cup butter
⅔ cup sugar
1 egg, well beaten
¼ cup brandy

Beat butter with sugar (to a cream, with an electric beater or by hand). Add a well-beaten egg. Heat in double boiler, stirring till thick. Add brandy before serving.

Lemon Sauce

Shortall Family Recipe

Makes about 1 cup.

½ cup sugar
1 tablespoon cornstarch
1 cup boiling water
2 tablespoons butter
1½ tablespoons lemon juice

Mix sugar and cornstarch and add the boiling water gradually, stirring all the time. Boil 5 minutes after it is well mixed. Remove from fire, add butter and 1½ tablespoons lemon juice. Stir till well blended. Very nice with gingerbread (see recipes, pp. 188–89).

Honey Love Sauce

Makes 1 cup.

½ cup walnuts
1 strip angelica
6 seeded raisins
4 maraschino cherries
1 cup strained honey
Juice of ½ lemon (2 tablespoons)

home of John and Frances Glessner. To these affairs he often brought famous guest musicians who were performing with the symphony, and it was at one of these dinners that world-famous pianist Ignace Paderewski informed Mrs. Glessner with pride that he "understood English fluently."

The Chicago Daily Tribune published a cookbook in 1877 that contained the following recipe, entitled "How To Get Fat," from the kitchen of Mrs. Sophia F., Chicago: "Take the yolk of 1 egg and 4 teaspoonfuls of white granulated sugar; beat well and fill the glass with beer. It is an agreeable drink, and will make anyone what I am now getting to be—fat."

Mrs. Glessner's many talents included the art of beekeeping. At the Glessner summer home in New Hampshire, she presided each season over the management of hives and the extraction of the harvest. In one banner year, the efficient operation

204 / ICE CREAMS, SAUCES

yielded 1,500 pounds of flower-scented honey, much of which was taken home to Prairie Avenue, where it found its way into the pantries of friends. At Christmastime, jars of the prized delicacy were distributed to the wives of police officers as part of the seasonal largesse to the local constabulatory.

1 tablespoon sherry or rum
Whipped cream and cherry to top (optional)

Chop walnuts, a thin strip of angelica, seeded raisins, and maraschino cherries; add strained honey to which lemon juice has been added. A tablespoon of sherry or rum makes an added improvement. Pour mixture over vanilla ice cream. Heap a tablespoon of whipped cream on top and decorate with a cherry.

Modern Cooking Tip: Angelica is available in health food stores' herb section.

Prairie Avenue Household Formulas and Hints

No Victorian cookbook could have been complete without a vast selection of household recipes for such cleaning products as laundry soap, hand soap, furniture and silver polishes. Commercial products for household cleaning tasks were available, but they were expensive, suspect, and difficult to obtain in small communities or remote towns. Just as today, the circulation of homemade solutions for household cleaning tasks was commonplace. Here I quietly leave my readers on their own, since these recipes have not been tested. At the very least I hope they will amuse, and at most they might even provide a useful solution for some housecleaning needs. Although doubtless a challenge to modern readers, they give us all a greater understanding of, and respect for, the complexities of dealing with seemingly simple household chores at a time before no-wax floors, self-cleaning appliances, enzyme-laden laundry detergents, and permanent press stain-resistant fabrics.

Cold cream: 1 ounce of rose water; ½ ounce of spermacetti; 1 drachma of white wax, and 14 drachmas of almond oil. Melt the last three in a china cup, on hot water; then add the rose water gradually.

Hard soap (Anderson family): 2 quarts clean grease (strained); 1 can lye dissolved in 1 quart cold water; 1 cup ammonia, and 2 tablespoons borax dissolved in cold water (in earthen or iron vessel). Then add the dissolved borax and ammonia and stir until thick. Let stand overnight. Next day, cut into squares. Requires no cooking.

Aunt Lucy's yeast (Anderson family): 1 quart sliced raw potatoes. Boil in 3 pints water. Pour water into ½ cup flour, ½ cup sugar, ¼ cup salt. Stir all together, then mash potatoes, and add 5 pints cold water and add to other mixture. When it is lukewarm, take 1 yeast cake soaked in ½ cup lukewarm water. Stir all together. Put in a

35. Glessner House master bedroom.

warm place to rise overnight. In the morning, put in a cool place, closely covered.

Silver polish (Shortall family): 2 boxes electro silicon; 2 boxes silver white (if unavailable, use 1½ ounces infusorial earth and 1 ounce whiting) ½ cake Ivory Soap and 1 pint water. Boil till perfectly smooth.

Cleaning cloth (Anderson family): Shave fine 4 ounces Castile soap. Let soak overnight in 1 quart soft rainwater. In the morning, set on stove where it will melt, but not boil. Add 1 ounce of liquid ammonia, ¼ ounce spirits of wine, and 1 ounce of ether. Bottle the mixture and shake well. When using the cleaning fluid, dilute a small quantity with 4 times as much boiling water.

Washing silk: Mix together 1 tablespoon of molasses, 2 tablespoons of soft soap, and 3 of alcohol; add to this 1 pint of hot rainwater; lay your silk on a bare table and rub on the mixture with a small clothes brush. Have ready a tub of lukewarm rainwater; dissolve five-cents worth of white glue and put in the tub of water. As you clean each piece of silk, throw it in the water and let it lie until you have finished; then dip each piece up and down in the water but do not wring it. Hang it up to dry by the edges and iron it before it is quite dry.

Caring for a casserole: Rub a new casserole, inside and outside, with garlic, which tends to prevent cracking.

Washing dishes: Dinner dishes and plates that have had greasy food upon them may be rubbed off with a little Indian meal before putting into water. They are thus prevented from making the water unfit for continued use, and the meal, saved, by itself, is good for the pig or chicken, if you have them.

Onions without tears: Put a small piece of potato on the tip of the knife as you peel.

To keep red ants away: Leave pieces of gum camphor about where they come. They do not approve of it and will retire, leaving the camphor victor.

Photographic Credits

The author and publisher wish to thank the following individuals and institutions for kindly permitting us to reproduce the photographs in this cookbook.

Frontispiece. Photograph by Bob Shimer, Hedrich-Blessing Photographers.
1. Courtesy of the Chicago Architecture Foundation.
2. Courtesy of the Chicago Historical Society.
3. Courtesy of the Chicago Architecture Foundation.
4. Photograph by Bob Shimer, Hedrich-Blessing Photographers.
5. Photograph by Judith Bromley.
6. Photograph by Bob Shimer, Hedrich-Blessing Photographers.
7. Photograph by Bob Shimer, Hedrich-Blessing Photographers.
8. Courtesy of the Chicago Architecture Foundation.
9. Photograph by Abby Sadin, Sadin Photo Group.
10. Photograph by Bob Shimer, Hedrich-Blessing Photographers.
11. Courtesy of the Chicago Architecture Foundation.
12. Courtesy of the Chicago Historical Society.
13. Courtesy of the Chicago Historical Society.
14. Courtesy of the Chicago Architecture Foundation.
15. Courtesy of the Chicago Architecture Foundation.
16. Courtesy of the Chicago Historical Society.
17. Courtesy of the Chicago Historical Society.
18. Courtesy of the Chicago Historical Society.
19. Photograph by Bob Shimer, Hedrich-Blessing Photographers.
20. Courtesy of the Chicago Architecture Foundation.
21. Courtesy of the Chicago Architecture Foundation.
22. Courtesy of the Chicago Architecture Foundation.

23. Photograph by Bob Shimer, Hedrich-Blessing Photographers.
24. Courtesy of the Chicago Historical Society.
25. Photograph by Bob Shimer, Hedrich-Blessing Photographers.
26. Courtesy of the Chicago Architecture Foundation.
27. Courtesy of the Chicago Architecture Foundation.
28. Photograph by Bob Shimer, Hedrich-Blessing Photographers.
29. Courtesy of the Chicago Architecture Foundation.
30. Courtesy of the Chicago Architecture Foundation.
31. Courtesy of the Chicago Architecture Foundation.
32. Courtesy of the Chicago Historical Society.
33. Courtesy of the Chicago Historical Society.
34. Courtesy of the Chicago Architecture Foundation.
35. Photograph by Bob Shimer, Hedrich-Blessing Photographers.

Carol Callahan is curator of the Glessner House Museum in Chicago's Prairie Avenue Historic District. A social and decorative arts historian with thirteen years of museum experience, she has also taught architecture and decorative arts history at the University of Colorado and the University of Denver. She lectures widely on nineteenth-century architecture and decorative arts, is active in the Victorian Society in America, and has written numerous articles and contributed to several books on these subjects. She is currently writing a book on Glessner House.